S*** MY KIDS SAY

S*** MY
KIDS SAY

Nick Harris

MICHAEL O'MARA BOOKS

First published in Great Britain in 2012 by
Michael O'Mara Books Limited
9 Lion Yard
Tremadoc Road
London SW4 7NQ

A CIP catalogue record for this book is available from the British Library.

Papers used by Michael O'Mara Books Limited are natural, recyclable
products made from wood grown in sustainable forests. The
manufacturing processes conform to the environmental regulations
of the country of origin.

ISBN: 978-1-84317-867-5 in paperback print format
ISBN: 978-1-84317-981-8 in EPub format
ISBN: 978-1-84317-982-5 in Mobipocket format

1 2 3 4 5 6 7 8 9 10

Designed and typeset by Design 23
Illustrations by Andrew Pinder
Printed and bound by CPI Group (UK) Ltd

www.mombooks.com

CONTENTS

INTRODUCTION

Children are rarely short of something to say. In fact, just about the only time they do appear lost for words is when you ask them something along the lines of 'Why did you flush Granny's false teeth down the toilet?' And even then they're back in full flow once they've thought up some excuse, invariably delivered with absolute conviction.

That's the thing about kids: they're so sure that their version of events – and indeed of the world in general – is right. So when they state that dinosaurs died out because they smoked too much, or that the Queen lives in an igloo outside Manchester, they do so with such certainty that you're almost ready to believe them.

In this collection kids give full rein to their unique and forthright views on everything from God to Uncle Ted's piles. As well as discussing such topics as kissing, weddings, family, school, ambitions, pets, Santa and poo, they also demonstrate with a selection of hilarious exam clangers that they don't always get things right. Let's face it, it's all good practice for when they become adults.

POWERS OF LOGIC

Constantly focused on a repetitive round of eating, playing and sleeping, kids would have you believe they've got little going on upstairs ... think again.

OUT OF THE MOUTHS OF BABES

Kids regularly belie their tender years by coming out with inappropriate remarks that would make Ricky Gervais blush.

I wish someone we knew would die so we could send lots of flowers.
ALICE, SEVEN

Dad, why are those men carrying that long box on their shoulders? What's in the box? Is it their fishing rods?
JARVIS, FIVE

Why are they burying Uncle John deep in the ground? I thought you were supposed to go to heaven after you die, but it looks as if Uncle John's going in the other direction!
GERI, SIX

All the folds of skin on the back of that man's neck
make it look like a pack of hot dogs.
BILLY, FIVE

Is that Mr Robertson's nose or is he eating a banana?
CHRISTOPHER, FIVE

See that lady in the red dress? Gee, she's big. I didn't
know you could get dresses that big!
WAYLON, FIVE

If your bra size is thirty-four, Mummy, that lady over
there must be size 120. Her boobies are huge!
ERIN, SIX

My mummy's fat because she's having a baby.
What's your excuse?
GINA, SEVEN

That man has a patch over his eye. Does that mean he's
a pirate? If so, where's his parrot?
JAMES, FIVE

Are you the lady from number thirty-four, the one
Mummy says breeds like a rabbit?
NATALIE, FIVE

☺

Are you going to go on Jerry Springer to find out who
your baby's father is?
WILMA, SIX

☺

Are you the lady in our street who used to be a man?
CLARISSA, FOUR

I don't understand how you can start off as a man and
then become a lady. What happens to all your dangly
man bits? And which toilet do you have to go in, or is
there a special one for people who are half and half?
MELANIE, SEVEN

Mum says the lady next door is approaching sixty, but
she doesn't say from which direction.
SIMON, EIGHT

If your sister hits you, don't hit her back.
They always catch the second person.
NATHAN, EIGHT

I didn't know ladies could have a moustache. Cool!
JUSTIN, SIX

Grandma, we've been waiting in line here forever behind
that lady. It takes Daddy less time to poop and he's in
there long enough to play a world of Angry Birds!
JANE, SIX

Mummy, why are old people always so slow?
Wouldn't it be better if they just died?
PHYLLIDA, FIVE

When people get to fifty I think they should just be killed off
to make room for all the new babies. It would stop the world
getting too crowded. If I was God, that's what I would do
anyway. But I'd let you and Daddy live a bit longer — maybe to
fifty-five — if you did me burgers for tea every Friday.
CHARLIE, SIX

STRAIGHT FROM THE HORSE'S MOUTH

This party is as flat as a witch's tit. I heard my dad say that once but I don't know what it means exactly.

GARRY, SIX

Nathan and me are just going out to play. We're going to hump some girls.

ALEX, FIVE

Ben and me are going round to Rob Henry's house because Rob's a really good laugh and people say his big sister's a great shag ... Mum, what's a shag?

DAVID, EIGHT

We had a vote in class today to see who was the most popular girl. I gave Miranda Hartley five out of five. My friend Jamie gave her one.

GARETH, SIX

When me and Sarah went to the seaside in the summer holidays, we hid in the sand dunes and watched my big sister doing it with her boyfriend. It was fun.

LAUREN, SEVEN

Mum, look at that man's funny nose. He looks like Bert from *Sesame Street*.

SEAN, FOUR

What's that horrible smell? It smells like my brother's butt in here!

ANDRE, FIVE

I was just about to eat a bogey and there was a hair in it. That's so gross!

BRITNEY, FIVE

What do I want for tea? A bowl full of bogeys. They're my favourite food.

ROXIE, FOUR

WISE BEYOND THEIR YEARS

Kids may not know how to keep their room tidy or how to play with plasticine without getting chunks of it stuck in their hair, but they are capable of imparting words of wisdom worthy of any philosopher.

If you can't remember how old you are, Grandma,
you must look in the back of your panties.
Mine say five to six.
MELANIE, FIVE

Are you sure that's a pool of petrol in the driveway,
Mum? I thought it was a dead rainbow.
BECKY, SEVEN

Climate lasts a long time, but the weather is only
a few days.
JUSTIN, SIX

HOW TO HAVE AN EASIER LIFE

Never laugh at your dad if he's mad or screaming
at you.
ROGAN, TWELVE

When your dad is mad and asks you, 'Do I look stupid?'
don't answer him.
BILLY, SEVEN

When your mum is mad at your dad, don't let her brush
your hair.
SUSANNAH, EIGHT

Never tell your mum her diet's not working.
MICHAEL, NINE

No matter what you do, your mum can always tell when
you're lying.
JAMIE, FOURTEEN

✉

Beauty is skin deep, but how rich you are can last a long time.

CHRISTINE, SEVEN

✉

Oil pollution is dangerous. When my mum opened a tin of sardines last night, it was full of oil and all the sardines were dead.

EMILY, SIX

You should always give someone a compliment, especially your teacher, even if it's a lie and she is really the wicked witch.

KYM, SEVEN

Never talk back to a teacher whose eyes and ears are twitching.

ANDREW, NINE

The best time to do a fart is when you're in the bath. The smell is so bad it makes your eyes water. It's like the worst-ever stink bomb.

IVAN, EIGHT

When it gets dark it's because God turned out the lights
so he could sleep.
RICHARD, EIGHT

You shouldn't listen in on your sister's conversation
with her boyfriend because it gets too mushy.
MONICA, ELEVEN

Never tell your little brother that you're not going to do
what your mum told you to do.
JOSH, SEVEN

Never ask a two-year-old to hold a tomato.
SARAH, ELEVEN

When you get a bad grade at school, show it to your
mum when she's on the phone.
ALYESHA, THIRTEEN

When you want to stay home from school, you have to
stay in the bathroom a long, long time.
JOSEPH, ELEVEN

PRANKS, JOKES AND LESSONS IN NAUGHTINESS

You should never underestimate a small child's ability to get into more trouble.
ANN, FIFTEEN

Never dare your little brother to paint the family car.
MARK, TEN

It isn't the best thing to dump a bowl of ice cream over your brother's head — no matter how mad you are.
LAURA, TWELVE

You can play the coolest tricks when people don't know that you have a twin.
AMIE, FIFTEEN

Never ask for anything that costs more than $5 when
your parents are filling out tax forms.
CAROL, NINE

When you want something expensive,
ask your grandparents.
EDWARD, TEN

Never tell your friends your parents' nickname for you
or you'll never hear the end of it.
DAWN, THIRTEEN

If you live with five other women, you have to get up
bright and early to get into the bathroom.
MEGAN, THIRTEEN

Don't try out your new chemistry set near where your
mum's making a cake.
COLLEEN, ELEVEN

When you and a friend buy ice cream cones, your
friend's flavour always looks better.
AMANDA, FOURTEEN

Forget the cake, go for the icing.
CYNTHIA, EIGHT

You shouldn't put a marshmallow in the microwave.
MARY, TWELVE

When your mum says, 'Try it, you'll like it,'
you probably won't like it.
EMILY, TEN

To be a real woman, you have to be really bossy
without looking bossy.
SIMONE, EIGHT

It's best not to use felt-tip markers for lipstick.
BECKY, SEVEN

Stay away from prunes.
JOHN, FIVE

Beware of cafeteria food when it looks like it's moving.
ROB, TEN

If there is something bad for dinner, your parents don't
have to eat it but you do.
DEANNA, ELEVEN

You can't fake a stomach ache right before you're
having spinach for dinner.
JESSICA, ELEVEN

You can't hide a piece of broccoli in a glass of milk.
RORY, SEVEN

A person should take a bath once in the summer,
not so often in winter.
FRANKIE, SEVEN

If Mum's not happy, nobody's happy.
KATY, THIRTEEN

A piece of chewing gum stuck under the dinner table will
one day return to haunt you.
DARREN, THIRTEEN

Never try and open an umbrella in the car.
RYAN, SEVEN

Don't lick a car bumper in winter.
OLLIE, NINE

Never spit when you're on a roller coaster.
SCOTT, ELEVEN

You should never jump out of a tree using trash bags
as parachutes.
APRIL, TEN

Never complain to your mum that you're bored, because
she will tell you to go and clean your room.
JOANNA, THIRTEEN

IT'S ALL
RELATIVE

Kids are at the centre of their own worlds, but
that doesn't stop them from waxing lyrical on
Dad's bodily functions, annoying little sisters or
Grandma's wrinkles.

MUMS AND DADS

For most children, their mums and dads are the most cherished things in the world – except of course for ice cream, new trainers, an expensive bike, a trip to Disneyland and the latest must-have video game.

Mum, if you have a baby growing in your tummy, what's growing in your bottom?

TESS, FIVE

Mum, why do you have two boobies? Is one for hot milk and one for cold?

JAMES, SIX

Mummy, why do you have big boobies when Daddy only has little ones?

CAITLIN, FOUR

I didn't recognize you in that picture,
Mum. Wow, you used to be so pretty!
KELLY, FIVE

Mum, you have lovely teeth.
Yellow is my favourite colour.
JENNY, FIVE

Mummy, why do you have those lines on your face?
KATIE, FOUR

Mummy, your hair looks brown.
You need to put some yellow in it.
ABI, FIVE

Mum, why are your armpits so hairy?
Are you turning into a werewolf?
JOEY, SEVEN

Mum's hair looks funny first thing in the morning.
It sticks out everywhere. She looks like a cockatoo.
SAM, EIGHT

My mum has hairy legs that she shaves with a machine.
JAKE, EIGHT

Mummy, your hair looks like fur. But it's not fur, is it?
STEPHEN, FIVE

My mum's hair is blonde but it's all black at the bottom.
I think that must be the soil on her head that her hair
grows in.
ANGELA, FOUR

On holiday, my mum went water skiing. She fell off
when she was going very fast. She says she won't do
it again because water fired right up her ass.
JULIE, SEVEN

You won't fit on that chair, Mummy.
Your bum is too big. You'll break it.
ZOE, FOUR

I liked Mum's hair better when it matched her eyebrows.
KEVIN, FIVE

You're not really fat, Mum. You've just got more flesh
than most people.
KAREN, SIX

Dad and I were talking, Mum, and we think you need
to go to the gym.
JOSH, SEVEN

Darryl's mum works out twice a week and she's pretty
fit ... for a mum.
KIERON, NINE

Jamie's mum is the hottest of all the mums who come
to school. Next time I see her, I could ask her to give
you some tips if you like — you know, about clothes
and stuff.
SEBASTIAN, NINE

Face it, Mum, the only things that are hot about you
these days are your flushes.
TONI, FOURTEEN

I think my mum is pretty even though she does have a neck like a turkey.

PAULA, SEVEN

My mum is very pretty although sometimes she misses with her lipstick.

ALEXA, EIGHT

Sometimes I think my mum dresses a bit frumpy, but I guess she is thirty-two, which is really old.

ANGELICA, NINE

When we're out together, my mum wears shorter skirts than me, and it's so embarrassing. I say to her, 'Mum, no one wants to see your forty-five-year-old thighs.'

LAUREN, FOURTEEN

I like my mum to look like a mum, not someone who's on the pull.

ADAM, THIRTEEN

Our car doesn't have a roof, so Mummy drives
around topless.
REBECCA, SIX

Mummy, how come you have way more shoes than I
do?
BONNIE, EIGHT

Mummy wears lots of cardigans even though Daddy
says they make her look old. When he says that, she
threatens to hit him with a rolling pin, but she never
does — except one time when her hand slipped.
JENNIFER, SEVEN

So they make you beautiful by sucking the fat out of
your butt? Who has to do that? What kind of a job is
that? Do they swallow it or spit it out?
EMILIA, SEVEN

Why do you want to change the way you look, Mummy?
Not everyone can be beautiful.
SORSHA, SIX

TIME TO GIVE MUM SOME SPACE ...

My mum is kind but gets mad if I try to talk to her
while her favourite soap is on TV.

BETHANY, SIX

My mum got angry once when the cat was
sick in her slipper and she didn't know till
she put it on.

SYLVIE, SEVEN

My mum loses her temper when people knock on the
door and try to sell her things. She says they're some
kind of witness, but I don't know what they're supposed
to have seen.

SHONA, TEN

Mum gets cross with me when I don't eat all my dinner.
But I've told her a zillion trillion times: I hate Russell
spouts!

JACK, FIVE

God made Mum just like he made me.
He just used bigger parts.
PHOEBE, FIVE

God makes mothers out of clouds and angel hair and
everything nice in the world and one dab of mean.
LIAM, SIX

My mummy loves me more than anybody. You don't see
anyone else kissing me to sleep at night.
JANINE, EIGHT

Mum, can you kiss this hurt spot? I need kissing all
over, but don't worry, I'll keep my pants on.
MICHAEL, SEVEN

My mum can spend two hours on the phone talking to
her sister, and when I ask her afterwards what they
talked about she says, 'Nothing.'
GERARD, ELEVEN

Sometimes my mum laughs so much that she wets
herself and has to rush upstairs to change her knickers.
KIRSTEN, EIGHT

Mum says I can't have any pudding unless I eat my dinner, but when I do eat all my dinner like a good boy and I ask if there's any pudding, she says, 'You can't still be hungry!'

DYLAN, EIGHT

My mum is a good cook but sometimes her gravy doesn't move and we have to help it out of the jug.

CERI, SIX

Mum's such a bad cook that Dad says our cat only has three lives left.

TOM, EIGHT

We always pray before meals, not because we're very religious but because Mum is such a lousy cook.

BRAD, TWELVE

My brother says our mum is the worst cook in the world. But I don't think that's fair. Michelle Higginbottom's mum is even worse.

ALISON, EIGHT

My mum picks her nose all the time and flicks it in the bin.
CARL, SIX

Mum bites her fingernails then tells me off for sucking
my thumb.
AIDEN, SIX

Mum chews her nails all the time.
She is almost down to her knuckles.
NOAH, NINE

✉

My mum has smelly feet, which she puts in my face.
The smell is so bad it knocks me off the sofa.
JAKE, EIGHT

✉

I think God made mums because they are the only ones
who know where things are kept.
STEVEN, SEVEN

Mummy, when you have your face lifted will it be on top
of your head, like a hat?
BECKY, FIVE

My mum does massive burps at the dinner table and in shops.

MAXWELL, SEVEN

My mum will eat a whole box of chocolates in one go — even the boring caramel cups.

ALICIA, NINE

Mummy, why are there more idiots on the road when Daddy's driving?

OLIVIA, SIX

My dad drives the same way on the road as he does on my Demolition Derby game.

JARED, TEN

My daddy has no hair on his head but some under his mouth. I think his hair must have slipped.

HAYLEY, FOUR

My dad brakes too hard in the car and his feet smell.

KATE, SIX

Other dads go for a haircut; mine goes for a
wax and polish!
DEAN, TWELVE

When Mum parks the car, Dad says, 'Don't worry, dear, I
can walk the rest of the way to the kerb.'
ALFIE, SEVEN

My daddy's got a giant bald patch on the top of his
head. Mummy says he looks like a monkey or is it a
monk? One or the other.
JEFF, SIX

My daddy's got no hair. He's bald, but not as bald as the
man across the road.
SIMON, FOUR

Dad doesn't usually get mad but when he does you'd
better watch out. He's like King Kong, only don't tell him
I said that or he'll get even madder.
NATHANIEL, TEN

Mum doesn't want to be boss, but she has to because Dad's such a goof ball.

HOLLY, EIGHT

Dad is hopeless around the house. He once put his shirt and dirty socks in the dishwasher.

VAUGHAN, EIGHT

When my daddy gets mad, steam comes out of his ears and nose holes.

CATHY, SIX

Dad's socks are disgusting. Mum says they have a life of their own and could probably walk to the washing machine.

ELLA, EIGHT

Dad can never understand why he often has an odd number of socks after Mum has washed them. To make his point he hops around the house on one leg like a mad pirate. Mum just rolls her eyes. She doesn't think he's at all funny.

ARIANNA, SEVEN

PARTY TIME!

Once my dad came home from the pub and fell flat on his face in the hall. He said he had tripped over the dog. But then Mum reminded him that the dog died two years ago. So he said he had tripped over where the dog used to lie. Mum just gave up and let him sleep it off for a few hours.

BRANDON, TEN

Dad always goes to the pub on the bus. He drinks fifty-nine pints and gets very drunk.

SAMUEL, SIX

Daddy always smells of the pub when he comes home. I'm worried that I might get drunk just by him breathing on me.

ZOE, EIGHT

I hope beer tastes better than it smells on Daddy's breath.

ANTHONY, SIX

DANCING QUEEN

Mum says the one thing my dad and the dog have got in common is that they can't dance because they've got two left feet.

JUSTIN, NINE

Dad thinks pointing at his ears is dancing.

MEGAN, EIGHT

Mum says when Dad dances he looks like he's having a fit.

CHRISTIAN, SEVEN

My dad thinks he can sing but he can't. The cat hides when he starts.

MELANIE, TEN

My mum's a nice singer but my dad sounds like a bullfrog.

DESTINY, SIX

My daddy eats way too much. He's got a tummy like a bouncy castle.

GRACE, FIVE

Dad snores so loud the windows rattle, and worse still Mum has to put on subtitles because she can't hear the television.

ISABELLA, NINE

My dad not only sounds like a farmyard, he does the smells, too.

GAVIN, NINE

My dad's got so many bad habits it's hard to say which is the worst. But Mum tells him off if he scratches his bum in the supermarket.

GABRIEL, SEVEN

Daddy's always reaching down the front of his pants to have a scratch. I don't know what he's got in there.

KAYLEE, FOUR

When my dad pumps, he never says, 'Pardon me!'

LACY, NINE

When my dad gets angry he keeps trumping.
He can't help it: fart, fart, fart. The smell in the room
is worse than his temper.

IAN, NINE

My dad has man boobs. Mum says he should wear a bra.

ELLIE, SEVEN

✉

Dad falls asleep on the couch and trumps. Mum does
ironing, shopping, cooking and everything, while my dad
just sleeps.

NIAMH, SEVEN

✉

It's bad enough that my dad trumps so much, but Mum
hates the way he waves it towards her with his hand.

MAISIE, SIX

When my dad does a pardon, he lifts his leg up and tells
everyone, 'That was better out than in.' He is so gross
sometimes.

SAVANNAH, TEN

When Dad goes in the bathroom, I listen outside the door for any plopping sounds. If I hear him say 'Hallelujah', I know it's gonna be a good time to ask him for more pocket money.

RYAN, EIGHT

When Dad goes to the toilet he often leaves little floaty ones behind.

JORDAN, SIX

If Dad's been more than ten minutes on the toilet, when he comes out he usually says, 'I wouldn't go in there for a while if I were you.'

LUIS, EIGHT

When Mum and Dad argue, if Mum isn't winning she just bursts into tears. It always works. Dad backs off after that and feels guilty. Women can be sneaky like that.

ROCKY, NINE

There's a difference, Dad: boys fart, girls toot.

SAM, FIVE

43

Mummy said Daddy was in the dog-house. But I looked,
and he wasn't.
MAISIE, FIVE

Dad is always in trouble over something with Mum. I
feel sorry for him sometimes. It's tough being a guy.
HENRY, SEVEN

If Mummy is angry with Daddy, he usually buys her a
box of chocolates, but he makes sure he gets to eat the
orange creams.
FAITH, SIX

Daddy says sorry to Mummy by picking her a lovely big
bunch of flowers from the garden but then she tells him
off again because he might be bringing greenfly into
the house.
MOLLY, EIGHT

Before she married my dad, my mum had to know his
background. Like is he a crook?
Does he get drunk on beer?
DAMON, EIGHT

I think my mum married my dad because she got too old to do anything else with him.
JESSIE, SEVEN

🌹

My mummy and daddy were both students at university and they fell in love at the degradation ball.
ALEX, FIVE

🌹

Mum and Dad met when they were in a stage play together. She was the front end of a horse and he was the back end. She says she's been cleaning up after him ever since.
EVAN, THIRTEEN

Mum said she married Dad because she wanted someone to sweep her off her feet and he was a street cleaner. It may be a joke.
SOPHIE, SEVEN

Dad says he married Mum because he couldn't afford to keep paying the train fare to go and see her at weekends. He's not very romantic.
I hope my husband's not like that.
CLAIRE, SEVEN

My grandma says that Mum didn't have her thinking cap on when she married Dad.

ERICA, SEVEN

Mummy, is that big moon in the sky the place where you and Daddy went after the wedding?

LEONIE, FIVE

Mummy, why are you and Daddy sleeping in separate beds? Does it mean your sex life is over forever?

EMILY, NINE

One night I went to ask Daddy for a glass of water and I found him on top of Mummy in bed. He was making strange grunting noises like a pig, so I decided to get the glass myself.

POPPY, SIX

I had a bad cough and went downstairs to get a drink of water in the middle of the night, and do you know what, Grandpa? I found Mummy and Daddy sunbathing in front of the gas fire.

ANTHONY, FIVE

My dad really gets annoyed when he can't get an Internet connection. His face goes all red and he looks like he's about to explode like an exploding thing.

CALLUM, SEVEN

The only thing that annoys my dad is if he finds there are no more beers in the fridge.

SCOTT, NINE

My big brother says I should sneak in and take a photo of Mum and Dad when they're at it and post it on the Internet. He says they'd love it, but I'm not so sure. I think he could be trying to get me into trouble.

JAMES, SEVEN

I caught Mum and Dad doing it one night. It didn't look much fun. I hope I never have to do things like that.

PETER, EIGHT

Mummy, why were you inflating Daddy last night? Had he gone flat?

ANNEKA, FIVE

SIBLING RIVALRY

Kids simply love doing things with their brothers and sisters. Particular favourites are pinching, squeezing, scratching and gouging as well as selling them to the Bogey Man.

✉

Mum asked me what I wanted for my birthday. I said, 'To be an only child again.'

MATTHEW, THIRTEEN

I'd like to strangle my brother with something like a rope or a python so I can have his bed.

JAKE, FIVE

I love playing football with my brother, but Mum says it might damage his head.

MATTHEW, THIRTEEN

My brother whistles in his sleep. It's like sharing a room with a kettle.

RAVI, NINE

Big brothers are good for stopping you getting bullied at school. There must be other things that are good about them but I can't think of any.

SHANE, SEVEN

My big brother always has to sleep in the top bunk, which is so unfair. If he farts in the night I'm afraid it's going to land on my face.

ROBBIE, EIGHT

If all boys are like my annoying brother, I'm never going out with one. I think I'll become a nun instead because then I won't have to go on dates or do kissing.

SAMANTHA, SEVEN

I hate sharing a bed with my brother because he's fat and greedy. Not only does he take up most of the bed but I worry that he's going to eat my pillow.

KYAL, SEVEN

I love birds, I love animals, I love fishes, I love trees, I love mountains, I love rivers, I even love insects and worms. In fact, I love everything in the world except my brother, who's a proper little shit.

SIAN, TEN

Dad says Trouble is my brother's middle name. But it's not really, it's Nigel. If I had a choice, I think I'd prefer to be called Trouble.

ALEXANDER, NINE

My little brother's dirty diapers are even worse than liver!

MATT, ELEVEN

My brother's acne is so bad, my sister and I hold him down and play 'join the dots' on his face with a marker pen.

INGRID, THIRTEEN

Sometimes I have nice dreams about my brother, but mostly they're about nailing his head to the floor.

RAMON, ELEVEN

My brother's top of the class at everything, good at sport, can play the piano and always does his homework on time. And he's got a girlfriend. I hate him.

MANISH, EIGHT

The main reason I don't like my brother is because he got bought a new pair of trainers before me. I expect I'll forgive him one day in about 150 years.
BOBBY, EIGHT

I don't understand how so many of my friends can fancy someone who used to wet his bed.
MAXINE, NINE

I hate my brother because he's teacher's pet, but not like my hamster, although he does belong in a cage.
RACHEL, SEVEN

My brother's always borrowing my skateboard without asking. It's so rude. All he has to do is ask me, and then I could say 'no' to his face.
CALEB, NINE

I've got three brothers and two sisters, which means I never get much of my own birthday cake.
BRADLEY, SEVEN

THE WRINKLIES

Grandparents can play such an important role in a child's development. After all, who else is going to teach kids to swear, burp, fart and generally drive their poor parents crazy?

Grandparents don't have to do anything but be there when we come to see them. They are too old to play and run hard so they just take us shopping and buy us stuff we want.
HENRY, SEVEN

Grandma can never remember my name. She goes through all the boys' names she can think of beginning with R — Robert, Ronald, Roland, Rodney, Roy, Reggie, Randolph, Rudolph, Richard — before she finally gets to Rufus.
RUFUS, TWELVE

I think your grandparents are kind to you because we all share a common enemy — Mum and Dad!
ASHLEY, THIRTEEN

Grandparents are more fun than parents. Whereas Mum and Dad are always busy, busy, busy, Granny and Grandad have more time for you. I think they're just happy still to be alive at sixty.

KEIR, TEN

When Grandma and Grandad read to us they don't skip pages and they don't mind if we read the same story over and over again. Or maybe they've forgotten that we just read it.

KIM, SIX

Sometimes Grandma forgets things. But she's not the only one. Last month the Prime Minister came to our school and asked the class, 'Do you know who I am?' So I guess he has trouble too.

HARVEY, SEVEN

🌹

My grandma says she's nearly sixty, but I don't know that number. I only go up to ten.

LEILA, THREE

🌹

Are you sure you're only fifty-two, Grandma? Your face
has a lot of wrinkles.
JENNY, SEVEN

My friend Jimmy said he didn't think you looked old enough
to be a grandma. I told him, 'Don't worry, she's old enough.'
DEXTER, EIGHT

Dad, there's a man at the door collecting for the old
folks' home. Shall I give him Grandma?
JONTY, SIX

I think you're getting younger, Grandma. You have black
hair coming out of your grey hair.
LEONA, SIX

Grandma, why are you taking your teeth out? You're not
going to take your eyes out, too, are you?
NAOMI, FIVE

My granny's got bingo wings but she can't fly.
SHAUNA, SIX

GRANDMA, WHAT LOVELY TEETH YOU HAVE

I once found Grandma's teeth in a glass at the side of her bed. Mummy wouldn't let me try them on though.

KITTY, SIX

Grandma's got a lovely smile, except when she takes out her false teeth.

ZOE, EIGHT

I saw my grandma's false teeth on her bedside table. They looked like they belonged in a museum.

OLLIE, NINE

It says on the news that there are metal thieves about, so should we keep Grandma indoors in case someone tries to steal her new hip?

SIMON, EIGHT

✿

Grandma warns me not to step on the cracks in the pavement because bears will come out and get me. I don't think it can be true because surely the bears would want someone bigger to eat like Mr Jenkins next door.

GABBY, FOUR

✿

Hey, Grandma, Mummy says if your butt gets any bigger we'll have to put a 'Wide Load' sign on it.

BILLY, EIGHT

Grandma Natasha has a lot of hair on her top lip. Daddy calls her Granny Tash.

MYLEENE, SIX

I mustn't hug Grandma too tight because sometimes when I do it makes her pee on the floor.

ROBERT, FIVE

My grandma talks funny, so I can't always understand everything she says. But she's still lovely. In fact, Granny Lisp is my favourite grandma.

ELIJAH, NINE

Hey, Grandma, why don't you and Grandpa have names like the rest of us?

ARTIE, SIX

If Grandma's got a frog in her throat, does that mean she's going to croak?

PATRICK, EIGHT

Grandma's not looking very well, is she? Do you think she'll have to be put down?

JADE, FIVE

Grandma can never hear me when I talk to her on the phone. I don't think she listens loud enough.

PAULA, SIX

My friends think my grandma is really cool. Grandad says that's because she's got bad circulation.

ALICE, SEVEN

Granny lives near a graveyard, which is good because when she dies they won't have far to take her.

SLAVIA, NINE

Mummy, the giraffe house at the zoo was disgusting. It smelled like Grandma.
ALISON, FOUR

It's funny when Grandma and Grandad bend over because they have gas leaks but they blame the dog for them.
JIMI, SEVEN

Mummy, you know how when you buy food at the supermarket it has a sell-by date? Do people have them too? Is Grandma past her sell-by date because sometimes she smells a bit off?
VERONICA, EIGHT

I wonder what it's like in heaven. You'll be there soon, Grandma, so you can tell me.
OLIVIA, FOUR

Grandma, I can smell something ... and I think it's you.
DEBORAH, FIVE

Is it OK for you to buy green bananas, Grandma? Aren't you worried that you'll be dead before they're able to get ripe?

MILES, SIX

Why are you sending me to my room?! All I said was Grandpa smells of wee. I didn't know it was a secret.

JAMES, SEVEN

My grandpa doesn't work any more — he's retarded.

JENNY, FIVE

I love Grandpa because he smells of the old days.

NATASHA, SIX

Life wasn't very nice when my great-great-grandad was alive. There were no aeroplanes, no computers, no cars, no telephones, no clean toilets, no cures for lots of diseases and no *Strictly Come Dancing*.

PHILIPPA, NINE

We've been learning about oxygen at school. Was oxygen invented before or after you were born, Grandad?

LORNA, SIX

Grandma, how come Grandpa is so grouchy and mean at home but so nice and quiet when we go to restaurants?

SOPHIE, FIVE

Sometimes Grandpa forgets to pull up the zip on his trousers and Grandma says to him, 'Norman, the beast is asleep but the gate is open.' I don't know what it means, but it always makes Mummy and Daddy laugh.

ALEXIS, SEVEN

Before my grandad was born there were no cars, and so people rode horses everywhere. It must have been hard getting the horses to stop at traffic lights.

MIRANDA, SIX

I heard Grandpa say a rude word while he was out in the garden. He paid me a dollar not to tell Grandma. I hope I hear him saying more rude words.

ZACHARY, SEVEN

ANOTHER DAY, ANOTHER DOLLAR

From a young age kids tend to have a clear idea of what they want to do when they grow up, no doubt shaped by their mum's persistent demands to help out around the house and their unique take on the jobs their parents choose to do.

THE WORKING DAY

Kids used to know what work their parents did. Mum would sit around at home all day drinking coffee while Dad would go to the office and pretend not to sit around all day drinking coffee. But times have changed ...

My daddy goes to work, but he doesn't actually do any work — he just eats biscuits and plays on the computer.

MARIELLA, FIVE

If Daddy's job is to go to work and my job is to go to school, then what's your job, Mum?

LOUISE, NINE

I'm not sure what my dad does but he must be very clever because whenever anything happens at work they say he's responsible.

WILLIAM, EIGHT

Daddy spends his day with his head down other people's toilets. He's something to do with plums.

LESLEY, SIX

I don't know what my daddy does at work but I think he has his own chair, so he must be important.

TAMSIN, SIX

My dad catches the train to work every morning. He says he spends the whole journey smelling other people's armpits and their garlic breath.

JOHN, TWELVE

I went to my dad's office once, and there were lots of people just sitting around all day doing nothing. Dad said they're called managers.

PAUL, TEN

My daddy is in the army. He's a sergeant. He has three stripes, which is more than a lance corporal but not as many as a tiger.

HELEN, EIGHT

My dad mends people at the hospital. If any of their body bits fall off, he glues them back on. He's a sturgeon.

AHMED, SIX

My dad works for a big bank in the City of London, but he says if anyone asks what he does for a living I should say he slaughters defenceless animals because it's less embarrassing.

PHILIP, ELEVEN

❀

Daddy's job makes him very tired. I can tell because he skips pages when he reads me a bedtime story.

FELICITY, FIVE

❀

Daddy was so tired after work one day that when I read the bedtime story he fell asleep! I woke him by throwing a glass of water over him because I'd seen how that worked on *Tom and Jerry*. I've also seen Jerry hit Tom in the face with a frying pan, but I don't think I'd better try that with Daddy.

DANIELLE, SIX

My dad always said hard work never hurt anybody ...
until he sliced off the top of his finger in the chainsaw.
ALVIN, EIGHT

Dad's a builder. Mum says he improves everybody else's
house but never ours.
FRED, TEN

My dad interviews celebrities for a magazine. He has to
ask them lots of difficult questions, like 'Do you believe
in dragons?'
KEVIN, SIX

Dad says he has two bosses — one at the office and
one at home. I think he's more scared of the one at
home.
TOBY, THIRTEEN

My dad is a funeral director. Mum says she's glad he
doesn't bring his work home with him.
HENRY, NINE

WHEN I GROW UP

All kids dream about what they want to be when they get older – whether it's discovering a cure for cancer or running their very own nail bar.

When I grow up, I want to be a police officer so I can arrest people and take them to jail, especially my cousins, who are buggers.

ADAM, SEVEN

When I grow up, I want to be a doctor so I can open Mum up and make sure she's OK inside. But I'll remember to close her again afterwards.

JASON, FIVE

When I grow up, I want to be the most famous golfer in the entire world — more famous even than Tiger Woods. I had my first lesson last week.

MARK, TEN

I want to be a traffic warden so I can stop people parking in the wrong place and hand out lots of fines.
LINDSEY, SEVEN

When I grow up, I want to be the captain of a big ship and have lots of sailors.
VALERIE, SIX

I want to be a nurse so I can make people better and take babies out of people.
MEGAN, FIVE

I want to be a dentist so I can look in people's mouths all day and see what they've had for dinner.
CARRIE, EIGHT

I want to live on a tropical island, where I can eat coconut, be surrounded by beautiful women and play on my Xbox all day.
HARRY, ELEVEN

When I grow up, I want to be bigger than I am now so I don't keep getting picked on.
NIKHIL, SEVEN

THE SKY'S THE LIMIT!

One day I want to climb Mount Everest, but it will have to be on a day when my mummy won't mind if I'm home late for tea.

SAMUEL, SIX

When I grow up, I want to be an astronaut with my very own rocket. I could fly it to the corner shop to get Mum's bread and milk.

TIM, SIX

When I grow up, I want to be invisible. Because then Mum will never know where I am, so she won't be able to tell me off or ask me to help clear the dinner table. And I'll be able to sneak up on girls and kiss them without them knowing who it was. Also I can creep out of the house and go to my friend Michael's house where we can drink milk shakes all night long. Do invisible people have mouths?

GAVIN, EIGHT

When I'm older, I want to live in a big house with a Rolls-Royce, a swimming pool, a butler, a maid, a private cinema and a hot dog van. And at the weekend we'll go out and shoot ducks and peasants.

BARNEY, NINE

I want to be able to beat my dad at chess because he never lets me win. I'll always let my kids win at things but my dad is mean. Last night he took my king in three minutes. I think he was in a bad mood because Mum made him do the dinner dishes.

ALEC, EIGHT

When I grow up, I want to be Michael Jackson.

EDWIN, FIVE

When I'm older, I want to kiss Kirstie Edwards in Miss Rickman's class.

KEIRAN, FIVE

When I grow up, I want to be a head teacher so I can get my own back on Mr Bailey, my PE teacher.

JOEL, ELEVEN

When I grow up, I want to be the first person ever to swim all the way round the world. And I'll do it without water wings.
PETER, FIVE

I don't ever want to die. I want to be immoral.
ANDY, EIGHT

I want to swim with dolphins — but not in a race.
BEN, NINE

When I grow up, I want to be a Transformer, so I can change into anything I want, like a cheetah or a Ferrari.
JAMES, EIGHT

When I grow up, I want to drive a fast car and sound my horn at all the other drivers, like my dad does.
JOHNNY, TEN

I want to work on the fast checkout at a supermarket, so if I see anyone with more than seven items in their shopping trolley I can call the police and have them taken away to be thrown in jail and whipped.
RUTH, EIGHT

MOTHER'S LITTLE HELPER

Kids would rather listen to Grandpa's stories about rationing and the good old days than help Mum around the house. So if they appear deep in thought after you've asked them to do a chore, they're probably trying to come up with a good reason for getting out of it.

✉

But, Mum, if I clean up my room, that means I have to do work, and you and I both know kids aren't allowed to work.
WILSON, SEVEN

But if my room is tidy, I just don't get the feeling that someone is living there.
GARETH, SEVEN

But if my room was tidy you wouldn't think I'd been busy.
ANNETTE, NINE

HOME HELP

There's a good reason why I didn't clean my shoes and as soon as I think of one I'll tell you.

JAMES, EIGHT

I did clean the bathroom. But then Dad went in and left his mark.

JACKSON, TEN

Sometimes I help Mummy with the hoovering, and Daddy helps by lifting up his legs.

JENNI, SIX

My teacher said slavery was abolished almost 200 years ago, but it's still going on in our house!

OLLIE, NINE

But, Mummy, I'm worried that if I dust my room I might
make some spiders homeless.
JODIE, FIVE

I can't clean my room, Mum, because I have developed
an irrational fear of dust.
SHANE, TWELVE

You found a chocolate biscuit under my pillow? I
wondered what had happened to that.
FRANKIE, EIGHT

But, Mum, you can't expect me to clean my room again.
I only did it last year.
DINO, EIGHT

But my room is tidy! It's just that things are arranged
in an unconventional manner.
CIARAN, FOURTEEN

The reason my underwear is all over the floor of my room
is because the Panty Fairy came and left me presents.
AISLING, SIX

What's the point in hanging up my school uniform? I'll
be wearing it again in two weeks.
RUDI, NINE

I can't tidy my room because right now I'm Spiderman!
ALEX, FOUR

I did clean my room, but it just got dirty again.
ETHAN, SEVEN

But, Mum, if you take into account all the homework
I've done this week, tidying my room would amount to
overtime and I'm not sure that you and Dad can afford
to pay me that.
CHARLIE, TWELVE

I'm too dizzy to tidy my room just now. Maybe tomorrow.
PHILLIP, SEVEN

If I do clean my room, what's in it for me? I need to
know what kind of deal is on the table.
FRED, THIRTEEN

CLEVER CLOGS

If it's not a constant barrage of questions, then it's a dazzling array of original answers to exam questions – kids have a unique and sometimes insightful take on the world.

QUESTIONS, QUESTIONS

Kids have an endless supply of baffling questions, which they usually save up either for bedtime or for when Dad is listening to the football results.

If God created heaven and earth and stuff, who created God? Was it Father O'Flynn?

BERNADETTE, FOUR

If God is good, why does he allow horrible things to happen like plagues, floods, droughts and Aunt Nora coming to stay?

JENNY, SEVEN

Do you think God makes bad things happen because he's in a bad mood — perhaps because he's lost at cards to St Peter?

ALEX, SIX

If God is good and kind, why did he let my hamster get sucked up the vacuum cleaner?

KITTY, SEVEN

Do you think God ever has days when he thinks, 'Oh, I can't be bothered. I'll just let the world run itself today'?

GEMMA, EIGHT

Does God sit up there in a giant control room in the clouds controlling everything that happens on earth? Or does he sub-contract the work out to mini-Gods in different countries, a bit like Uncle Jim's building firm?

ALVIN, TEN

Dad, did God make us in China?

EMMYLOU, FIVE

If God moves in mysterious ways, is he like the knight in chess?

STEPHEN, EIGHT

Why is it called lipstick if you can still move your lips?

EMMA, TEN

HOW STUFF WORKS

Dad, what is puke made of?
KYLE, SIX

Why is sick so pretty but it smells disgusting?
VERONICA, FIVE

Are there many calories in snot?
JENNIFER, SEVEN

Why is snot green?
ALEX, FOUR

Dad, why do I have a belly-button?
JOSHUA, SIX

Why do I have earwax in my ears?
AHMED, SIX

Why don't they make mouse-flavoured cat food?
RACHEL, EIGHT

Can mute people burp?
PATRICK, TEN

My jumper shrunk in the wash, so why don't sheep
shrink when it rains?
HAYLEY, EIGHT

When you die, do you stay dead forever and ever and
ever? Or do you come back a few years later after you've
had a nice rest as a duck or a caterpillar or something?
MIA, EIGHT

Why does a cowboy wear two spurs? If one side of the
horse goes, surely the other side does too?
STU, ELEVEN

If Jesus was so smart, why didn't he think to turn
water into oil?
RUDI, TWELVE

If you die and come back as another person, how come you don't remember any of your previous life? You could once have been a Roman centurion, Dad, but nowadays I bet you can't drive a chariot.

JAMIE, EIGHT

If today is the first day of the rest of our lives, what was yesterday?

SELINA, ELEVEN

Why is it that when you blow in a dog's face he gets mad at you but when you take him in a car he sticks his head out of the window?

CARL, NINE

How do chickens get inside eggs and how come when we cook an egg a chicken doesn't come out?

LAURA, SEVEN

Who counts the pollen for the pollen count and how long does it take them each day?

GEORGE, EIGHT

How come I've got straight blond hair but there are often short, dark curly hairs on my bar of soap?
OSCAR, SEVEN

How do 'Keep off the Grass' signs get where they are?
JERMAINE, SEVEN

If a rabbit's foot is so lucky, what happened to the rabbit?
ANGUS, EIGHT

✉

If swimming is good for your figure, why are whales so fat?
KAREN, NINE

✉

Why do they call it 'after dark' when really it is 'after light'?
ROB, EIGHT

If you jogged backwards, would you gain weight?
JOSS, TEN

Why is she called Mother Superior when she doesn't
have any children?
NIAMH, SEVEN

Is it true that nuns always walk in pairs and that if you
see a nun by herself she's an imposter? Someone told
me that.
GUY, NINE

If superglue can stick everything, why doesn't it stick
to the inside of the tube?
HELENA, ELEVEN

When cheese gets its picture taken, what does it say?
DARREN, SIX

Why do dogs sniff other dogs' bottoms to say hello?
Why don't they just bark in their face?
TAMSIN, SIX

Daddy, why do you like looking at pictures of naked
ladies?
LILLIAN, FIVE

SCHOOL DAYS

Ah, the best days of our lives, or so we are told. But it never seems like it at the time, what with school dinners, crusty old teachers, irregular verbs, cross-country running, bossy prefects and simultaneous equations.

My sister's in a class of her own — but only because she has nits.
JESSICA, ELEVEN

Miss, what do you mean my shoes are on the wrong feet? I know for sure these are my feet.
HARRY, FIVE

My teacher told me off for passing notes to Jimmy at the back of the class. But we weren't passing notes. We were playing cards.
ROBBIE, ELEVEN

I like Mrs Johnson. She is our teacher. I like it when
she does meths with us.

CHARLOTTE, FIVE

You can get away with the best stuff when you have a
substitute teacher.

KEVIN, EIGHT

My teacher said she was pleased my handwriting has
improved because now she can see how bad my spelling is.

DERMOT, SEVEN

Dad, my teacher said I'm going to be famous. He said
one more stunt like I pulled today and I'm history!

WAYNE, EIGHT

Why am I doing my maths homework on the floor?
Because the teacher told us not to use tables.

MARTIN, SEVEN

Sorry, miss, my baby sister ate my homework. She ate
tomorrow's homework too.

SABINA, SEVEN

TEACHER, TEACHER

I don't think our teacher knows much. All she does is ask us questions. She's a teacher, she ought to know the answers.

JEREMY, SIX

The teacher said I have listening problems, but I think she has problems teaching.

MOHAMMAD, SEVEN

Mum, how many times do I have to tell you that it's not my fault if I don't learn anything? It's the school's problem if they're not going to teach me anything.

BRADLEY, SEVEN

It's not my fault that I got bad marks at history. The teacher keeps asking about things that happened before I was born.

NEIL, NINE

I was doing my homework in the bank while waiting with my mum, but then the bank was robbed by a masked man with a gun and he made me hand my homework over.
KENNY, EIGHT

I couldn't do my maths homework, miss, because I have a solar-powered calculator and it was cloudy all weekend.
KENNETH, NINE

I didn't do my homework because I heard on TV about someone who was shot dead because he knew too much. I don't want to take that risk.
FRANKIE, EIGHT

Sorry, sir, I left my homework in my other shirt and my mum put that shirt in the wash this morning.
ROLAND, TWELVE

On the way to school a sudden gust of wind blew my homework out of my hand and I never saw it again.
TIM, TWELVE

I don't have my homework, sir, because my family just got a new paper shredder. I had to try it out and I accidentally shredded my homework.

JOHN, TWELVE

I did my homework on the computer but my dad thought I was messing around so he deleted it as a joke.

DAVID, ELEVEN

I saw a boy in a lake, so I dived in to rescue him but my homework drowned.

CHARLIE, TEN

Last night I got temporary amnesia and I totally forgot about my homework.

PHILIP, TEN

I always put aside an hour to do my homework but this was the weekend the clocks went forward, so I lost that hour.

MASON, TWELVE

My kitten died and I didn't have any paper to wrap him in, so I had to use my homework.

LACEY, NINE

Well, sir, I was abducted by aliens outside the library last night and they only just let me go, so I didn't have time to do my homework.

MATTHEW, TWELVE

Sorry I don't have my homework with me, sir, but my mother thought it was so good she's taken it into town to have it framed.

ZAK, ELEVEN

I did my homework but on my way to school I saw a dog dying of starvation. So I fed it to him.

GAYE, TWELVE

DAD'S FAULT

Sorry I didn't do my homework but last night my dad and I got into a big row about who was the best teacher in school. I said you were, sir.

ROBERT, NINE

I don't have my homework because my dad, not realizing what it was, scribbled a rude word on it while he was on the phone to his boss.

STANA, TEN

My father had a nervous breakdown and he cut up my homework to make paper dolls.

SOL, ELEVEN

I couldn't do my homework, miss, because while washing my hair I got shampoo in my eyes and was blinded for the rest of the evening.

GEORGIA, NINE

It's against my religion to do homework on a day ending in 'y'.

PRIYA, TEN

The dog was about to do a big poo on our new lounge carpet and we couldn't find any newspaper, so I had to put my homework down instead. I didn't think you'd want it after that.

JORDAN, TEN

Dad, this is hopeless. You've spent two hours on this one maths problem. Unless you start improving, I'm going to have to ask someone else to do my homework in future.

JORDAN, ELEVEN

Sorry I'm late for school, miss, but I saw a sign along the road. It said, 'School Ahead, Go Slow.'

CHRIS, EIGHT

COUGH, COUGH

I wasn't here yesterday because I had student flu — I was sick of school.

CARTER, TEN

I couldn't come to school yesterday, miss, because I was in bed with Gramps.

FLORENCE, EIGHT

Mum, I can't go to school today, I have the hiccups. And if I go to school with the hiccups, then all my friends will get the hiccups.

KYLE, SIX

Mum, can I have a diarrhoea? All the other kids in school have got one so they can write down their homework.

EMMA, SEVEN

Sorry I'm late, miss, but my foot fell asleep and I didn't want to wake it up.

SANJEEV, NINE

I was late for school because there are eight kids in my family and my mother set the alarm for seven.

PATRICK, EIGHT

I'm late for school because my sister fused the house with her hair dryer last night and my alarm clock was reset.

MAXINE, NINE

I wasn't late — I thought the start bell was a fire alarm. I've been standing outside for twenty minutes waiting for the 'All Clear'.

WILL, EIGHT

Sorry I'm late, miss, but I accidentally squirted the toothpaste too hard and I've spent all morning getting it back in the tube.

NICOLE, ELEVEN

YOU KNOW WHAT I MEAN

Exams and tests can be a stressful time for students of all ages, which perhaps explains why these youngsters' answers were so spectacularly wrong.

ENGLISH

A census taker is a man who goes from house to house increasing the population.
LAURA, EIGHT

Philatelists were a race of people who lived in biblical times.
CHRIS, NINE

When a man is married to one woman, it is called monotony.
DAVID, SEVEN

Trigonometry is having three wives at the same time.
KELVIN, SEVEN

An epistle is the wife of an apostle.
CHRIS, NINE

A senator is half horse, half man.
BENJAMIN, EIGHT

A myth is a female moth.
ANNA, SIX

An executive is the man who puts murderers to death.
SAM, SEVEN

A troubadour is a Spanish bullfighter.
DAN, NINE

A tantrum is a bicycle for two people.
SIMON, EIGHT

A diva is a swimming champion.
MARIE, SIX

Steroids are things for keeping carpets still on
the stairs.
MELVYN, TEN

GEOGRAPHY

A fjord is a Scandinavian car.
JAKE, EIGHT

A virgin forest is a forest where the hand of man has
never set foot.
KIERAN, SEVEN

In some Asian countries, the people ride about in
jigsaws.
NATHAN, EIGHT

People go about Venice in gorgonzolas.
AIMEE, SEVEN

The Pyramids are a range of mountains between
France and Spain.
WILL, EIGHT

Most of the houses in France are made of plaster of Paris.
KERRY, SEVEN

Parts of the Sahara Desert are cultivated by irritation.
CHLOE, TEN

People who live in Moscow are called Mosquitos.
GEORGE, SEVEN

The Tropic of Cancer is a rare and dangerous disease.
BRADY, SEVEN

The four seasons are salt, pepper, mustard and vinegar.
JENNY, FIVE

Equinox is a country in South America.
JENNIFER, NINE

The climate is hottest next to the Creator.
CHARLIE, FIVE

The Matterhorn was a horn blown by the ancients
whenever something was the matter.
HARRY, EIGHT

Floods from the Mississippi may be prevented by putting
big dames in the river.
SHANE, SEVEN

HISTORY

The Greeks invented three kinds of columns —
Corinthian, Doric and Ironic.
ASWAD, ELEVEN

Socrates died from an overdose of wedlock.
BEN, EIGHT

There were no wars in Greece as the mountains were
so high that they couldn't climb over to see what their
neighbours were doing.
DEAN, NINE

The Romans were so-called because they never stayed
long in one place.
KYLIE, EIGHT

At Roman banquets the guests wore garlic in their hair.
MIRIAM, SEVEN

A gladiator is something that keeps a room warm.
EVE, SIX

Julius Caesar extinguished himself on the battlefields
of Gaul.
ABI, EIGHT

Nero was a cruel man who tortured his subjects by
playing the fiddle to them.
PENNY, SEVEN

Rome was overthrown by invasions of the Huns,
Visigoths and Osteopaths.
MURPHY, THIRTEEN

Christianity was introduced into Britain by the
Romans in 55BC.
LISA, ELEVEN

King Arthur lived in the age of Shivery.
SANJEEV, SEVEN

The Magna Carta proved that no free man should be
hanged twice for the same offence.
DOMINIC, THIRTEEN

Henry VIII found walking difficult because he had an
abbess on his knee.
NICK, SEVEN

Queen Elizabeth knitted Sir Walter Raleigh on the deck.
MAYA, SEVEN

Henry VIII's first wife was called Catherine the
Arrogant.
SASHA, EIGHT

After his divorce from Catherine, Henry VIII married
Anne Boleyn, and Archbishop Cranmer consummated the
marriage.
FELIX, ELEVEN

Edward VI of England could not rule alone because he
was a miner.
GEOFFREY, FOURTEEN

Sir Francis Drake defeated the Spanish Armadillo.
MICHAEL, SEVEN

Sir Francis Drake said, 'Let the Armada wait. My
bowels can't.'
BHARAT, EIGHT

When Queen Elizabeth I exposed herself before her
troops, they all shouted, 'Hurrah!'
TIM, EIGHT

In the sixteenth century, explorers like John Cabot and Martin Frobisher searched for America's back passage.
DANIEL, TWELVE

Oliver Cromwell had a large red nose, but under it were deeply religious feelings.
MIA, EIGHT

The sun never set on the British Empire because the British Empire is in the east and the sun sets in the west.
CHARLENE, FIFTEEN

Queen Victoria sat on a thorn for sixty-three years. She was the longest queen.
LIZZIE, SEVEN

Queen Victoria's death was the final event that ended her reign.
ELEANOR, TWELVE

William Tell invented the telephone.
KARL, SIX

Joan of Arc was burned to a steak.
PHILIP, ELEVEN

FRANCE AS YOU DIDN'T QUITE KNOW IT

The Edict of Nantes was a law passed by Louis XIV
forbidding all births, marriages and deaths in France for
a period of one year.
HANNAH, SIXTEEN

 Louis XVI was gelatined.
FIONA, FOURTEEN

During the French Revolution poor people were called
'Sans-Culottes' because they couldn't afford underwear.
ANTHONY, FOURTEEN

The French Revolution was caused by overcharging
taxis.
JAKE, NINE

Charles de Gaulle was named after Paris's airport.
RICHARD, ELEVEN

Karl Marx was one of the Marx brothers.
JO, ELEVEN

Grosse Bertha was Hitler's cleaning lady.
ADAM, THIRTEEN

Christopher Columbus circumcised the world with forty-foot clippers.
SEAN, SEVEN

😈

One of the nastiest Nazis was Joseph Gerbils.
JARED, TWELVE

😈

The Natchez Indians rose up and massaged all the French at Fort Rosalie.
CHELSEY, TEN

In the middle of the eighteenth century, all the morons moved to Utah.
ZOE, FIVE

Abraham Lincoln wrote the Gettysburg Address while travelling from Washington to Gettysburg on the back of an envelope.
LUKE, EIGHT

LITERATURE

SHAKESPEARE WAS BORN IN THE YEAR 1564, ON HIS BIRTHDAY.
JODIE, FIFTEEN

Shakespeare lived in Windsor with his merry wives.
PAUL, FOURTEEN

Romeo and Juliet are an example of a heroic couplet.
LOUIS, SEVEN

Romeo's last wish was to be laid by Juliet.
CHERYL, FOURTEEN

Writing at the same time as Shakespeare was Miguel
Cervantes. He wrote *Donkey Hote*.
TYRONE, TWELVE

✉

Homer wrote *The Oddity*.
KYLE, ELEVEN

✉

Charles Dickens was famous for his *Little Dorrit*.
ELLIOTT, THIRTEEN

MUSIC

Johann Bach wrote a great many musical compositions and had a large number of children. In between, he practised on an old spinster, which he kept in his attic.

DECLAN, FOURTEEN

Sherbet composed the *Unfinished Symphony*.

ZAK, ELEVEN

Handel was half German, half Italian and half English.

EVA, TEN

Beethoven was so deaf he wrote loud music.

CONNOR, TWELVE

Beethoven expired in 1827 and later died from this.

ANDY, TWELVE

Most composers do not live until they are dead.

MARLON, NINE

A song sung by two people at the same time is called a duel.

ALFIE, FIVE

A virtuoso is a musician with high morals.
ISAAC, TWELVE

If people sing without music, it is called Acapulco.
SHEREE, SEVEN

The principal singer of nineteenth-century opera was
called pre-Madonna.
LEROY, FOURTEEN

Refrain means don't do it.
LINDSEY, ELEVEN

Just about any animal skin can be stretched over a frame
to make a pleasant sound once the animal is removed.
DENZIL, EIGHT

RELIGION

Moses led the Hebrews to the Red Sea, where they made
unleavened bread, which is bread without any ingredients.
DIRK, SEVEN

The seventh commandment is thou shalt not admit adultery.
JASON, SIX

Moses wandered lost in the dessert for forty years.
ANNETTE, SIX

Moses went up on Mount Cyanide to get the Ten
Commandments.
SARAH, EIGHT

The people who followed the Lord were called the
twelve opossums.
MIKEY, SEVEN

☙

**David was a Hebrew king who was skilled at
playing the liar.**
JEM, NINE

☙

Solomon, one of David's sons, had 500 wives and
500 porcupines.
TESS, SIX

Lot's wife was a pillar of salt by day, but a ball of fire
by night.
LANCE, SEVEN

NEW BEGININNGS

When the three wise guys from the East arrived, they found Jesus in the manager.
RAMON, SEVEN

Jesus was born because Mary had an immaculate contraption.
TOM, SIX

Joseph and Mary took Jesus with them to Jerusalem because they couldn't get a babysitter.
NADINE, SEVEN

Samson slayed the Philistines with the axe of the Apostles.
CHARLIE, SIX

Noah's wife was called Joan of Ark.
ELROY, NINE

SCIENCE

Marie Curie did her research at the Sore Buns Institute in France.
PRESTON, ELEVEN

A vacuum is a large empty space where the Pope lives.
NANCY, EIGHT

Vacuums are nothings. We only mention them to let them know we know they're there.
LEON, NINE

Madame Curie discovered radio.
SHONA, SEVEN

One horsepower is the amount of energy it takes to drag a horse 500 feet in one second.
BAILEY, SEVEN

A vibration is a motion that cannot make up its mind which way it wants to go.
LUCY, TEN

One of the main causes of dust is janitors.
JAMES, SIX

Iron was discovered because someone smelt it.
ANDREW, EIGHT

The law of gravity says no jumping up without coming
back down.
KITTY, SEVEN

Cyanide is so poisonous that one drop of it on a dog's
tongue will kill the strongest man.
DAMIEN, TEN

A molecule is so small it cannot be seen by the naked observer.
BRYONY, THIRTEEN

✉

Electric volts are named after Voltaire,
who invented electricity.
SAMUEL, FOURTEEN

✉

When you smell an odourless gas, it is probably
carbon monoxide.
JESS, FIFTEEN

A super-saturated solution is one that holds more than
it can hold.
ROBERT, TWELVE

THE WONDERS OF THE HUMAN BODY

Blood flows down one leg and up the other.
DAVID, NINE

The alimentary canal is located in the northern part of Indiana.
LINDSAY, ELEVEN

The spinal column is a long bunch of bones. The head sits on the top and you sit on the bottom.
MARCUS, SEVEN

The skeleton is what is left after the insides have been taken out and the outsides have been taken off. The purpose of the skeleton is something to hitch meat to.
ADRIAN, EIGHT

To most people solutions mean finding the answers. But to chemists solutions are things that are still all mixed up.
MAX, EIGHT

Some oxygen molecules help fires burn while others help make water, so sometimes it's brother against brother.
FERNANDO, NINE

In looking at a drop of water under a microscope, we find there are twice as many Hs as Os.
DAN, TEN

H2O is hot water and CO2 is cold water.
MILES, NINE

Flirtation makes water safe to drink because it removes large pollutants like grit, sand, dead sheep and canoeists.
STEFAN, ELEVEN

We say the cause of perfume disappearing is evaporation. Evaporation gets blamed for a lot of things where people forget to put the top on.
LILY, EIGHT

The process of turning steam back into water is called conversation.
PAUL, EIGHT

Louis Pasteur found a cure for rabbis.
TOM, TEN

Archimedes was in the bath when he suddenly shouted, 'Ulrika!'
ALISTAIR, TWELVE

Water freezes at 32 degrees and boils at 212 degrees. There are 180 degrees between freezing and boiling because there are 180 degrees between North and South.
BEN, TWELVE

The earth makes one resolution every twenty-four hours.
STEVIE, NINE

The moon is a planet just like the earth, only it is even deader.
CARLY, SIX

Clouds are high-flying fogs.
JENNA, FIVE

Most books say our sun is a star. But it still knows how to change back into a sun in the daytime.
AMBER, SEVEN

Some people can tell what time it is by looking at the sun. But I have never been able to make out the numbers.
TRACEY, NINE

When people run around and around in circles we say they are crazy. When planets do it we say they are orbiting.
SIOBHAN, NINE

The wind is like the air, only pushier.
TRACEY, SEVEN

I am not sure how clouds get formed, but the clouds know how to do it and that is the important thing.
MATTHEW, EIGHT

Clouds just keep circling the earth around and around and around. There is not much else to do.
JESSICA, FIVE

PROVERBS

Unable to think of anything else to do on a Friday afternoon (and conscious World War Three might break out before the bell went) a bored junior school teacher gave her students the first lines of proverbs and asked them to complete the rest.

The pen is mightier than the . . . pigs.
JOEY, EIGHT

Two's company . . . three's the Musketeers.
SAM, EIGHT

If you lie down with dogs you'll . . . stink in the morning.
WAYNE, EIGHT

Don't bite the hand that . . . looks dirty.
MIKEY, EIGHT

Where there's smoke, there's . . . my mum's dinner.
JAMIE, EIGHT

An idle mind is ... the best way to relax.
RAYMOND, SEVEN

If you can't stand the heat ... get a pool.
KATRINA, EIGHT

A bird in the hand is ... safer than one overhead.
PETER, EIGHT

Happy the bride who ... gets all the presents.
NIAMH, EIGHT

You get out of something what you ... see pictured
on the box.
JENNIE, EIGHT

When the blind leadeth the blind ... get out of the way.
DEXTER, EIGHT

Laugh and the world laughs with you, cry and ... you
have to blow your nose.
SOPHIE, EIGHT

Don't count your chickens ... eat them.
BOBBY, SEVEN

Strike while the ... bug is close.
JAMES, EIGHT

There are none so blind as ... Stevie Wonder.
KIA, EIGHT

Too many cooks ... are on TV.
SAM, EIGHT

People in glass houses shouldn't ... run around naked.
MIKEY, EIGHT

Never underestimate the power of ... termites.
NELL, EIGHT

It's always darkest before ... Daylight Savings Time.
KENNY, EIGHT

A miss is as good as a ... mister.
JENNIE, EIGHT

LIFE'S PLEASURES

Kids have their favourite things; whether it's animals or Christmas, naturally they have a unique take on each!

MY FAVOURITE THINGS

With aunts to kiss and vegetables to eat, life can be a bitch even when you're only five years old. So it's always good to have something to look forward to.

My best friend is Ben but sometimes he breaks up with me 'cos he calls me names like 'Burger Face'.

LIAM, SIX

My favourite cousin is Kimberley. But that's only because I hate my other cousin.

ANDREAS, SEVEN

My favourite auntie is Auntie Renee because she doesn't make me eat the crusts on my pizza.

DAISY, SIX

My best friend is Matthew. He gives me money to tell people he's my best friend.

KENNY, SEVEN

My best friend is Simon. We always hang around together except in class where the teacher makes us sit apart.

AFZAL, TEN

My favourite uncle is Uncle Peter. He's good at football, tennis, table tennis and cricket. And he can wiggle his ears.

DANIEL, SIX

I like playing football in the park with my brothers. They're both tall so they make good goalposts.

ALLAN, SIX

I like going ice skating but I have to be careful because my dad warned me last week that I was skating on thin ice.

STEWART, EIGHT

I like going shopping with my mum. I will shop with her for hours and hours as long as I get a toy at the end of it.

JEREMY, SEVEN

My favourite movie is *Mission Impossible 4*, although I don't see how it can be impossible if they've done it four times already.

RICK, NINE

Blue is my favourite colour. Our car is blue, my summer dress is blue, the sky is blue, the sea is blue and Mum said the air was blue yesterday after Dad hit his thumb with a hammer.

JENNY, SEVEN

The best teacher at our school is our geography teacher Mr Jefferson because he tells jokes and forgets to set us homework. And he knows where Slovenia is.

STANLEY, ELEVEN

I like chicken nuggets but I don't know what part of the chicken the nugget is.

CARLA, SIX

My favourite subject at school is French. So now I know where all the wines that Mum drinks every night come from.

SUZY, ELEVEN

HIGH DAYS AND HOLIDAYS

My bestest holiday was when we went to Disneyland and I met Mickey Mouse. He's very big for a mouse.

ROSS, FIVE

I once went skiing with my school and that was my favourite holiday. The best bit was when my teacher, Mr Granger, fell and broke his leg. We had to leave him behind in Austria.

MELVYN, TEN

I like it when we go on holiday to Italy because I can eats lots of pizza and lots of ice cream. Sometimes I am a bit sick though.

GEORGE, EIGHT

I like going on holiday in our caravan and camping in a field because then I get to do a poo-poo behind the bushes.

PATRICK, FIVE

It's fun going on the slide in the park. And if you climb up behind a girl and stay back a bit you can sometimes see right up her dress!
ROHAN, SEVEN

Saturn is my favourite planet but I don't want to go there because they probably speak French.
DAVID, EIGHT

Bathtime is the best time of the week for me. I've got a big toy boat and I like to re-create the sinking of the *Titanic* by letting it crash into a sponge.
DARREN, EIGHT

I like talking to Grandma in Australia on the phone even though she doesn't understand everything I say. I think she's hard of thinking.
PIPPA, FIVE

I like to fart in the car and gross everyone out because it is funny.
KERRIN, SEVEN

JUNIOR JOKES

Why was the glow-worm unhappy? Because her children weren't very bright.

NICOLA, FOUR

What kind of snake would you find on your car? A windscreen viper.

JASON, FIVE

What do you call a Roman emperor with a cold? Julius Sneezer.

MELANIE, EIGHT

What did one plate say to the other plate? Lunch is on me.

MOHAMMED, NINE

What happens to ducks before they grow up? They grow down.

ROBERT, FIVE

What starts with T, ends in T and is full of T? A teapot.
NAOMI, SEVEN

What is brown, has four legs and a trunk? A mouse
coming back from vacation.
KYLE, SIX

Why did the pie cross the road? It was meat 'n' potato.
MAX, EIGHT

☺

What's a monster's favourite soup?
Scream of tomato.
HOWARD, SIX

☺

What's worse than finding a worm in your apple?
Finding half a worm.
ROBBIE, NINE

Why do elephants paint their toenails yellow? So they
can hide upside down in a bowl of custard.
GEORGE, EIGHT

THE MEANING OF CHRISTMAS

Mince pies, drink, tinsel, crackers, drink, mistletoe, turkey, more drink, Santa, hangovers – we all know what makes a real Christmas. But how do children see it?

Jesus was a king and he wore a crown even though he was a baby. It was a really small crown.

JAY, FIVE

I don't know what the three wise men brought Jesus but I would have given him a tin of biscuits. I think Mary, Joseph and Jesus would have all liked a biscuit.

DOMINIC, EIGHT

I don't know what presents the wise men brought Jesus but a Lego set would have been better.

WILLIAM, SEVEN

The three wise men brought Jesus gold, frankincense and myrrh. So no real presents. I feel sorry for him.

ELLIE, SIX

I know for his birthday Jesus got money and gold from the wise men but I would have given him a Liverpool kit.

DANIEL, SEVEN

At Jesus' birth there was a donkey, a sheep and cow there as well as Mary and Joseph. It sounds quite crowded.

HANNAH, SEVEN

There were sheep, horses and a crocodile outside the stable.

MATTHEW, SIX

The Angel Gabriel is a big white fairy. He helped Mary and Joseph look after the baby — kind of like a doctor.

ERIN, SIX

Gabriel was this herald angel. He was a boy but he's played by a girl in Christmas plays.

KATHERINE, NINE

DEAR SANTA . . .

I have been very, very good all year. I haven't done one thing wrong. So don't bother asking Mummy and Daddy if it's true.

LACEY, FIVE

I think I am worth a nice present this year because I have been very good. I have worked hard at school, I have been kind to my sister, I have helped Mum with the dishes, I have done my piano lessons and I have kept my room tidy. There was only the incident with the vacuum cleaner and the budgie but that wasn't really my fault.

CHARLOTTE, NINE

I have tried to be good this year, but my mum and dad tell me I'm not very good at it.

GEORGE, FIVE

I have tried very hard to be good this year but I have done some naughty things. I am sorry so don't listen to Auntie Vivian and still bring me my presents, please.

HARRY, SEVEN

I have been good until last night when the cat scratched me
and I was mad at it and thought I caught mouse disease.

MALLORI, SIX

I know you know where all the naughty girls live. So
please can you make sure that Emma Sykes of 3H is
on that list?

LORETTA, SEVEN

I am a good boy with an annoying brother so I think I
should get something big this year.

JEFFREY, SEVEN

I want to buy a spider in a pet shop, so tell me that
you'll come there and pay for it. The shop closes early
on Christmas Eve. Is that all right?

NATHAN, EIGHT

I didn't get the new bike I asked for last Christmas. So
I hope I'll be lucky this year. In case you can't find it
in your Lapland storeroom, it's got blue handlebars and
a black saddle and it needs to go to Peter Warner.

PETER, SIX

This year I'd like a helicopter for Christmas — not a toy one but a real one like my Uncle Karl. If that can't fit in your sack maybe you could bring me a Thomas the Tank Engine set.

ALED, SEVEN

I know I haven't been nice this year, but I promise to be next year. So would it be all right to give me something in advance?

JOSEPH, EIGHT

I'm sorry I was naughty this year but I can't help it if I get a really bad case of the grumpies.

CATHERINE, SIX

My birthday is on Christmas Day, so you have to remember to bring me two presents. I think it's only fair.

WILL, SIX

I want you to bring me a magic set, please, so I can make our teacher, Mrs Humphreys, disappear.

LUKE, SEVEN

Could you possibly make it so I can turn into a dragon?
ELISHA, FOUR

Last Christmas you brought me the wrong doll's house.
But I have forgiven you now. I hope you have better
helpers this year so you don't make the same silly
mistakes again.
BRIANNA, SIX

Please can you give me special powers like Superman?
If you can't do that, I'd like a new skateboard.
ADRIAN, SIX

All I want for Christmas is for my family to have a
good time. Oh yes, and please add chocolate to that.
ABI, SIX

Please can I have a pair of binoculars so that I can
see what my big sister and her boyfriend get up to
when he brings her home in his car?
MARY, SEVEN

THE INS AND OUTS

Do you say 'Ho! Ho! Ho!' because you don't speak other languages?

PAULINE, SIX

Do your reindeer eat lots of cabbage? If so,
I feel sorry for you having to sit behind their
butts all night!

VINCE, SIX

Do you have to clean up Rudolph's poo-poos? My dad
uses a bag when our dog poo-poos. Do you have bags?

CAITLIN, FOUR

You must spend a lot of money on sellotape. I hope you
can claim it back off the taxman.

RAOUL, SEVEN

Are Prancer and Dancer an item?

JODY, SEVEN

EVEN MORE QUESTIONS

What do you do for the rest of the year? Do you play golf like my dad?

ROWAN, SIX

Do you have just the one set of clothes? Who washes them for you? My mum can do it if you don't have a mum of your own.

MARIA, FIVE

Do you have to take your sleigh in to be checked over once a year? If so, don't take it to the garage on the corner of King Street because my dad says they rip you off.

JIMMY, SEVEN

When you're tired of being Santa, could I have your job? I am happy to come to Lapland for an interview.

JAMES, SIX

ALL CREATURES GREAT AND SMALL

Kids are endlessly fascinated by wildlife. How does a humming bird hover? Why doesn't an elephant ever forget? And which part of a baboon's anatomy reminds them of Grandma?

At Sunday school I learned that God named all the animals and you know what? He got them all right.
KYLE, SIX

penguins eat fish, but where do they get chips?
DANIEL, FOUR

Bears and hedgehogs hibernate and so does our laptop.
DANIEL, SIX

A camel's got legs like Tina Turner.
JASON, FIVE

My pet goldfish is named Bob because that's what he seems to say all day.
DAVID, SEVEN

All elephants are called Nellie.
GARETH, FOUR

Mummy says Daddy's like a bear with a sore head. But why do bears have sore heads? Is it because they drink too much beer like Daddy?
CHRISTINA, SIX

I like lions but I wouldn't want to keep one as a pet. I think the litter tray it would need might be too big for our kitchen.
SAMANTHA, SEVEN

Why do camels have their boobies on their back?
CAITLIN, FOUR

Camels store water in their humps. The hump must have
a lid so they can twist their neck and drink from it.
AIDAN, SIX

Camels froth at the mouth and spit. They're very rude.
And they don't wear a bra over their humps.
ERIN, EIGHT

I would only want to ride a camel if it had stabilizers.
AARON, EIGHT

One of the scariest snakes is the black member. It is
very long and can put you flat on your back in seconds.
AHMED, SIX

There is no known anecdote for a lot of snake bites,
which is why they are so dangerous.
JOANNA, THIRTEEN

I wonder what happens if a poisonous snake bites its own
tongue? I did it last week, but luckily I'm not poisonous.
JODIE, EIGHT

Daddy, is this fish called God?
MONICA, FOUR

It's cool the way snakes can shed their skin. Mum did that last summer after she got sunburned in Ibiza.
AIDEN, TEN

My pet snake eats mice. He doesn't like vegetarian pasta, though.
ROBERTA, SEVEN

My mum says the most dangerous snake in the world is the one-eyed trouser snake, but I can't find it in any of my wildlife books.
NOAH, SEVEN

I'm glad I'm not a mummy kangaroo, having to carry the kids around. It must be horrible for her in the school holidays when they're at home all day.
TAMZIN, SEVEN

A kangaroo keeps its baby in the porch.
ANNA, SIX

A STING IN THEIR TAILS

What's so special about a bee's knees?
They look pretty small to me.
PETER, SEVEN

Mummy, why do bees hum? Is it really because they
don't know the words like Daddy says?
LUCY, FIVE

I think God must have been having a bad day when he
created wasps.
THEO, SEVEN

I hate wasps because they always spoil our picnics. So
now we can't take fizzy drinks in case wasps come and
land on them and sting us. Wasps are so selfish. How
would they like it if we came along and wrecked their
fun days out?
JENNIFER, SEVEN

☘

Rabbits' poos look like currants. But they definitely don't taste like them.
SAM, SIX

☘

Why are they called pelican crossings? I stood at one for fifteen minutes yesterday and I didn't see a single pelican cross the road.
LAUREN, SEVEN

You wouldn't think something as ugly as a caterpillar could turn into something as beautiful as a butterfly. So I guess there's hope for my sister yet.
ELLIS, TEN

Anteaters have very long noses. I think my father must have been an anteater in a previous life.
AMELIE, EIGHT

Horses can run very fast — except the ones my dad bets on.
ADY, SEVEN

This is a picture of an octopus. It has eight testicles.
KELLY, SIX

Oysters' balls are called pearls.
JERRY, SIX

Sea lions can balance their balls on the end of their nose.
ABIGAIL, SEVEN

The ocean is made up of water and fish. Why the fish
don't drown I don't know.
BOBBY, SIX

At the zoo we saw a donkey with a big wanger. My dad
couldn't bear to look. He said nature was cruel.
ASHTON, EIGHT

Alligators are evil looking. They have mean
sneaky eyes like my brother when he is planning
something bad.
NATALIE, SEVEN

EIGHT-LEGGED MONSTERS

The female black widow spider kills the male after mating. I think she's got the right idea.
JULIE, TEN

There is a spider's web outside our kitchen window. It is very nice. But there are dead flies in it. I think the mummy spider needs to do more housework to keep her web tidy. My mummy would never have dead flies in her house.
DANNIELLE, SEVEN

How do spiders make webs? Do they knit like Grandma?
MHAIRI, SIX

Cygnets turn into swans, tadpoles turn into frogs and piglets turn into sausages.
JEREMY, SEVEN

Last week I saw one horse giving another horse a piggy-back in a field. Mummy said they were mating. So the next day when I saw Andrew Riley getting a piggy-back from his grandad I asked him if he and his grandad were mating.

DAVID, SIX

If racehorses are ridden by jockeys, who are small people, why don't greyhounds have little children riding them? It would be fun, and I could tell my greyhound not to waste his energy chasing that silly hare, because my dad says it is just a piece of cloth.

KIERAN, SEVEN

Mum, you know you said all birds and animals go to heaven when they die? Well, see that dead seagull lying in the road? Does that mean God threw it back down?

ALEC, SIX

Some big dinosaurs like the brachiosaurus only ever ate grass and leaves. With all that meat to choose from, why would they decide to eat vegetation all day? What a boring diet, and imagine how bad a brachiosaurus's farts must have been!

GEORGE, FOURTEEN

Chocolate milk comes from brown cows.
CORINNE, FIVE

If animals don't want to be eaten by people for food,
then why does their meat taste so good?
KATRINA, SIX

✉

I wouldn't want to go to Jurassic Park because I don't
think it has swings and a slide.
ELEANOR, FOUR

✉

Terry dactyl was a dinosaur that could fly. If it was
alive today, it could swoop down and snatch all the
naughty children in my class.
RACHEL, SIX

Dinosaurs had big bones. Mum says Auntie Brenda is big
boned, so that must mean Auntie Brenda is a dinosaur.
JACK, SIX

A leopard never changes his socks.
THOMAS, FIVE

LIFE LESSONS

From God and love to the world of the rich and famous and how on earth the human body works – it's impossible to shield kids from some of life's more challenging lessons.

THE BODY BEAUTIFUL

The workings of the human body are a mystery to most grown-ups, so children can't be expected to make head or tail of it, particularly all that business about how babies are made. If it's not done with Lego, it's far too complicated for young minds.

My mummy's got a baby in her tummy. I think the doctor put it in.

ADAM, FOUR

How did the baby get in your tummy, Mummy? Is it Daddy's fault again like the last one?

FLORENCE, FIVE

You make babies by taking all your clothes off. I took all my clothes off last night before I had a bath, so I hope I'm not going to have a baby soon.

SASHA, FOUR

Mummy, how did I get in your tummy?
Did you swallow me?
GEORGE, FOUR

**Making babies is something to do with the stork
and his pecker.**
CHRISTIAN, SIX

Babies are made by kissing — lots and lots of kissing.
So you have to make sure you suck a mint first or
you'll end up with a smelly baby.
RIA, FOUR

I've looked everywhere on my doll to see where babies
are made, but there are no directions. All it says is
'Made in China'.
ALICE, SIX

Men buy women flowers and chocolates, and nine
months later they have a baby. That's why Mummy won't
let me eat too much chocolate.
LUCY, FIVE

LESSONS IN PREGNANCY

It is easy to tell the make of a baby. If it's born blue it's a boy, and if it's born pink it's a girl.

PAUL, FIVE

The lady who lives next door is pregnant but I heard her say it was an accident. Can she call Claims Direct?

AMIR, NINE

Mummy, I do love you even when you are being sick, but can you please try not to sick my baby up?

MARTHA, FOUR

Mums can often get cross and crotchety when they're pregnant, but it's hard to tell with my mum because she's like that anyway.

JACOB, EIGHT

Mummies have babies through their bully button. Mine only has fluff in it.
LEWIS, FIVE

Do mummies who have twins need to have two tummies?
ERIN, FOUR

If the baby doesn't want to come out, the doctor climbs into the mummy's tummy and drags the baby out with his bear hands.
SUMMER, SIX

How does the baby come out, Mummy?
Do you poo it out?
LEANNE, FOUR

Sometimes if the baby won't come out, the doctor pulls it out with a pair of biceps.
PHOEBE, FIVE

When the baby comes out, there is always a nurse standing by to catch it.

ROSIE, SEVEN

Babies come out through a magic zip that appears on the mummy's tummy. You zip it open to get the baby out and then the zip disappears.

ANGEL, FIVE

When the baby is first born, it is attached to an umbrella cord.

LEAH, FIVE

Is it the postman or the stork who delivers babies?

ALEXIS, FIVE

An important person when the baby is born is the midwife. I don't know why they're called that. Is it because they're mid-way between a wife and a husband, like Mr Lucas at number seventeen who dresses up in women's clothes at the weekend?

ROGAN, EIGHT

I saw a drawing once of how babies are made. It doesn't look very easy. If I get a girlfriend, I think I might stick to shaking hands.

OLIVER, SIX

I'm never going to have sex with my wife. I don't want to be all grossed out.

THEODORE, EIGHT

Have a baby? Are you kidding? Have you ever smelled a baby's dirty diaper?

MARY-JO, EIGHT

I'm never having sex. I don't want anyone putting something disgusting inside me. It's bad enough having to eat broccoli.

CHLOE, ELEVEN

Having a baby looks gross, and anyway it wrecks your figure.

KAYLEE, TEN

I never want to have a baby. I don't want to have something growing inside me because I'd be scared that it would suddenly burst out of my tummy sending blood and stuff everywhere, like in a horror film.

SIENNA, SEVEN

I felt my baby brother kicking when he was inside Mummy's tummy. But I wouldn't allow any of that. I'd stick a Post-it note on my tummy saying, 'No talking after eight o'clock and no kicking!'

TIA, SEVEN

I can have two childs because I have two testicles.

EDWARD, SIX

Mum, why does my poo have bits of sweetcorn in it? I don't remember eating any.

ISAAC, SIX

Mum, what happened to Amy's penis? Did you leave it in your tummy?

ETHAN, FIVE

When women can't conceive a baby naturally, they have test tube babies. But I'm not sure how I'd get my willy inside a test tube — we use them in science lessons and they're not very wide.

GENE, ELEVEN

My baby brother has a tiny wiggle. Mine is medium, but you should see my dad's. It's ginormous!

JAKE, SEVEN

Boys have a penis and girls have a china.

LEWIS, FIVE

When I'm a big mister, I'm going to have a big willy like Daddy's.

KANE, FIVE

When you get old, so do your bowels and you get intercontinental.

SIMEON, SEVEN

My sister said I was fat. I told her they're my love handles. She said she was going away to be sick.

CARLOS, EIGHT

It's more than a tiny scratch on my face! How will I ever be chosen for *American Idol*? Simon will think I am hideous.

MICHELLE, SIX

My mummy says it's just a spot on my arm but I'm worried it might be a chicken pock.

SYLVIE, FOUR

✉

Does my school uniform make me look fat?

ELLA, FIVE

✉

I'd like to have different-coloured eyes. They're brown at the moment, but I really want blue eyes. I hope Mummy and Daddy will get me a pair of blue eyes for my next birthday.

AYSHA, FIVE

TEETHING TROUBLES

My two front teeth are crooked. My dad says they're good
for opening tins of beans.

STELLA, SEVEN

My tooth fell out three nights ago but still the Tooth
Fairy hasn't been. I hope she's not on strike.

EMMA, SEVEN

The dentist said I'm going to have a crown. I can't
wait! Will I get a throne too?

AYSHEA, SIX

The dentist's drill is just horrible. It is so scary.
I've seen what it's done to the road outside
our house.

TOM, SIX

My dad's got a bazooka on his foot.
ERIN, FIVE

Someone at school said Michael Geraghty has worms,
and I don't think they're his pets.
ISAAC, FIVE

When I broke my arm I had to have it in plaster for
weeks and weeks and weeks and everyone wrote nice
things on it except my brother who wrote 'Die, bitch.' He
was grounded for three months after that.
BRIDGET, EIGHT

Ben Stephens is my friend. We were playing doctors
and nurses one day until my mum stopped us because
he wanted to remove my appendix.
HANNAH, SEVEN

A girl at school had bugs in her hair. Soon the whole
class had them. Even the teacher was scratching like a
dog. My mum got rid of them by putting tar on my hair.
But it did mean I had to go to school smelling like our
garden shed.
JANIS, EIGHT

LOVE AND STUFF

When it comes to kissing and all that, kids today seem to fall into two categories: those who want to dive in straight away and those who are prepared to bide their time and wait, at least until they are potty-trained.

⚡

I would never put my tongue in a girl's mouth. It sounds disgusting, and besides I wouldn't want to taste her dinner.
DERMOT, NINE

Have you seen the disgusting things that boys put in their mouths? I wouldn't want to kiss one until I've checked for germs.
HELEN, SEVEN

You can learn to kiss by having a big rehearsal with your Barbie and Ken dolls.
JULIA, SEVEN

I would never kiss any boy who smokes cigarettes or eats broccoli.

GABRIELLE, FIVE

When is it OK to kiss someone? When they're rich.

PAM, SEVEN

When you kiss a boy you have to keep your eyes shut. If you keep them open it means that you'd rather be doing something else like painting your nails.

HANNAH, ELEVEN

I don't want any boy putting his tongue in my mouth, because I've just had new fillings put in.

KIRSTEN, TEN

When you kiss a boy it's a good idea to open your eyes halfway through just to make sure that his eyes are closed. If they're not, you can give him hell because he obviously doesn't love you.

SHELLEY, NINE

I learned to kiss by watching soap operas all day.

CARIN, NINE

THE TROUBLE BEGINS ...

I've only got one or two boyfriends. I don't want to marry any of them in case they are vampires.

MEGAN, FIVE

My boyfriend is Jake. He is always trying to kiss me. He has asked me to marry him. I said, 'yes' and hope to have forty-five children.

SAMANTHA, SIX

My boyfriend is Clyde. He's five and a half. My mum thinks he looks like David Beckham, but younger and with no tattoos.

ELLIE, FIVE

I've got a boyfriend called Kevin. He sometimes carries my box of crayons to play group for me. He's nearly five. My friends think he's a hunk.

JOSIE, FIVE

The first time I took a girl out, she suddenly collapsed and had to be rushed to hospital with appendicitis. It spoiled the date for me.

MARK, THIRTEEN

I've got 30 million girlfriends, but I can only remember one.

ADAM, SIX

Girlfriends aren't like pets. You can't just choose one. They have to choose you, too.

MITCH, SIX

I don't ever want a girlfriend in case she wants to get married during the football season.

JAKE, EIGHT

My girlfriend is a pain. She's just nag, nag, nag all the time. Why haven't you done your shoe laces up right? How did you forget to bring your PE kit? How have you lost your school dinner money?' I can't take much more.

ALFIE, EIGHT

I have a girlfriend at school called Laura and I love her,
but I'd still swap her for Cameron Diaz.
PETER, SEVEN

If you tell your best friend that you like a boy but ask
her to keep it secret, she tells the whole world.
MELISSA, THIRTEEN

My mother says to look for a man who is kind. That's
what I'll do — I'll find someone who is kinda tall and
handsome.
CAROLYN, EIGHT

It's worth learning the offside rule so you can impress
boys with how much you know about football.
WENDY, ELEVEN

❀

A great way to make a person fall in love with you
is to tell them that you own a whole bunch of
candy stores.
DEL, SEVEN

❀

DATING DOS AND DON'TS

On the first date, they just tell each other lies and that usually gets them interested enough to go for a second date

MARTIN, TEN

One kind of date is to take the girl out to eat. Make sure it's something she likes to eat. French fries usually works for me.

BART, NINE

A movie is a good place to take a girl on a date. That way you get to eat giant bags of Revels.

DAVID, EIGHT

Why is that you always get a zit when you've got a hot date?

LANA, TWELVE

The best way to get a boy to notice you is to help him
with his nine times table.
HARRIET, SEVEN

I've had a girlfriend for nearly two weeks, but she says
she doesn't want to get serious yet. So I think I might
dump her.
TOMMY, SIX

My friends keep telling me that to get a girl's attention
you should drop a live worm down her top. After that she'll
definitely go out with you, they say. But I'm not so sure.
JEROLD, EIGHT

Love is like an avalanche where you have to run
for your life.
JOHN, NINE

The way to attract a boy is to shake your hips and hope
for the best.
CAMILLE, NINE

I read in one of my mum's magazines that girls like boys who show their feminine side. Does that mean I have to wear one of my sister's dresses on a date?
WAYNE, SEVEN

If you want to learn to love better, you should start with a friend you hate.
TANIA, SIX

Love is that first feeling you feel before all the bad stuff gets in the way.
JENNY, EIGHT

⚡

Love is when a girl puts on perfume and a boy puts on shaving cologne and they go out and smell each other.
BILLY, SEVEN

⚡

Love is when my mummy makes coffee for my daddy and she takes a sip before giving it to him to make sure the taste is OK.
CHELSEA, FIVE

Love is when your puppy licks your face even after you
left him alone all day.
HOLLY, EIGHT

Love is when you tell a guy you like his shirt and he
wears it every day.
JENNY, TEN

Love is when one of the people has freckles and he
finds somebody else who has freckles, too.
ANDREW, SIX

Love is when someone hurts you and you get so mad
but you don't yell at them because you know it would
hurt their feelings.
NICOLA, SIX

Love is when Mummy gives Daddy the best piece of
chicken.
KEVIN, SIX

Love is what makes you smile when you're tired.
DANNI, SEVEN

Love is when you go out and give somebody most of your French fries without making them give you any of theirs.
ROBBIE, ELEVEN

Love is when Mummy sees Daddy smelly and sweaty and still says he is handsomer than George Clooney.
MARIE, TEN

Love is when Mummy sees Daddy on the toilet and she doesn't think it's gross.
AARON, FIVE

Love is when you still like someone even when they've got a scabby zit on their face.
KIRSTY, SIX

Love is when you don't break up with someone even if they don't like dark chocolate ice cream.
TOM, SEVEN

In a restaurant, lovers will just be staring at each other
and their food will get cold. Other people care more
about the food.

BRAD, EIGHT

You can tell when two octopuses are in love because
they walk arm in arm in arm in arm ...

JASON, EIGHT

People in love act all mooshy — like puppy dogs, except
puppy dogs don't wag their tails nearly as much.

ARNOLD, TEN

When you fall in love I think you're supposed to get
shot with an arrow or something, but the rest of it isn't
supposed to be so painful.

MANUEL, EIGHT

When someone loves you, the way they say your
name is different. You know that your name is safe in
their mouth.

MARY-LOU, SEVEN

You know someone loves you if they share the last
sweet in the packet with you.

LYNNETTE, EIGHT

People who are in love suddenly get movie fever so
they can sit together in the dark.

SHERMAN, EIGHT

Lovers hold hands to make sure their rings don't fall
off, because they paid good money for them.

GAVIN, EIGHT

✉

When someone says 'I love you', they're thinking, 'I really
do love him, but I hope he showers at least once a day.'

MICHELLE, NINE

✉

Love isn't always just about how you look. Look at me.
I'm handsome like anything and I haven't got anybody
to marry me yet.

BRIAN, SEVEN

Love is the most important thing in the world, but baseball is pretty good, too.

GREG, EIGHT

You got to be careful about who you marry. You got to find somebody who likes the same stuff. Like, if you like sports, she should like it that you like sports, and she should keep the chips and dip coming.

ALAN, TEN

Love? It gives me a headache to think about all that stuff. I'm just a kid — I don't need that kind of trouble.

KENNY, SEVEN

Twenty-three is the best age to get married because you know the person forever by then.

CAM, TEN

Men have to get down on one knee to ask you to marry them. It's the law. I've seen it in old movies.

KATHERINE, SIX

PLANNING THE PERFECT WEDDING

I want to go to my wedding in a helicopter like a member of the SAS on a special mission. The pilot could land in the churchyard, and we'd all have machine guns in case anybody in church objected to the marriage. Do you think they'd let me?

LENNY, EIGHT

I want to get married in Disneyland with Goofy as the best man.

LEANNE, SEVEN

I want to be married on a big bouncy castle by a vicar bouncing up and down.

MICHELLE, SIX

I love weddings. I want to have lots of them — at least twenty.

HARRIET, FIVE

It's not easy to tell if two people are married. You might have to guess, based on whether they seem to be yelling at the same kids.

DERRICK, EIGHT

Be a good kisser. It might make your wife forget that you never take out the trash.

ERIN, EIGHT

I'm in favour of love as long as it doesn't happen when *Sesame Street* is on TV.

CAROLYN, FOUR

I'll marry my husband through thickness and health.

GABBY, SIX

Marriage is when you get to keep your girl and don't have to give her back to her parents.

ERIC, EIGHT

It's better for girls to be single than boys. Boys need someone to clean up after them.

ANITA, NINE

THE RICH AND FAMOUS

You can guarantee that kids will know everything there is to know about the latest reality TV star, but how clued up are they on world affairs and people who are even more important than Simon Cowell?

I don't know what Queen Elizabeth does all day, but I think in the morning she orders people to be executed and then in the afternoon she watches *Cash in the Attic*

PETER, FIVE

Buckingham Palace is a big house, so the Queen must spend a lot of her time dusting and vacuuming. Because she's Queen, she's allowed to keep her crown on while she does it.

MAISIE, SIX

The Queen of England sits around on her throne all day ordering people, 'Get me some grapes.'

LUISA, FIVE

The Queen does all her own housework but she has a maid to do nasty jobs like cleaning the oven and washing Prince Philip's underpants.

JANETTE, SIX

Although the Queen is good at dusting she is only short. So she can't reach cobwebs that are high up on the ceiling. To get to them she stands on her throne.

BRITTANY, SIX

The Queen is very rude because she has ladies-in-waiting, and it's rude to keep people waiting.

HELEN, FIVE

The Queen has lots of corgis. I don't like corgis. They bite people and they're Welsh. When they bite Prince Philip, he bites them back.

ERIC, SIX

The Queen has to meet lots of people every day. They're allowed to shake her hand but they're not allowed to snog her.

FRANKIE, EIGHT

The Queen shakes so many hands her arms must be really strong by now. I bet she arm-wrestles Prince Philip.
MATTHEW, SIX

The Queen meets hundreds of thousands of people every day and has to shake hands with every one of them. That's why she always wears gloves because she doesn't want their sweat and grease on her.
SARAH, SIX

The Queen is nice. She smiles a lot. She only looks grumpy if Prince Philip has been naughty.
DONNA, FIVE

The Queen wears neat clothes. She looks very smart and sensible. She hardly ever dresses like Madonna.
KATY, SIX

Madonna goes to Africa and buys babies. Dad said she could have me for $50,000. I think he was joking.
FLOYD, SEVEN

The only person who is more powerful than the Queen in the whole world is God. I expect they're on the phone to each other all the time, planning what to do about the weather and Prince Harry.

NICHOLAS, SIX

Madonna is nearly ninety years old, but she is still able to sing a bit.

ABIGAIL, SIX

How do you annoy Lady Gaga? Poker face. My dad told me that joke.

SHAUN, EIGHT

Lady Gaga looks different every time I see her. That's why I think there may be more than one Lady Gaga, like it is with Santa at Christmas time.

TINA, SIX

Grandad calls Grandma 'Lady Gaga' because she is always forgetting things. She doesn't like it.

MILLICENT, EIGHT

POLITICAL ANALYSIS

The President of America lives in a white horse.
RYAN, FIVE

Americans have an erection every four years.
SAM, SIX

Americans choose a new President every four years.
They throw the old one out with the trash.
DUNCAN, SIX

The Prime Minister of England is David Cameron.
He is very posh and eats pheasant instead of
burger and fries.
NOEL, SEVEN

David Cameron lives at 10 Downing Street in inner-
city London. He probably can't afford somewhere nice
in the suburbs.
DANNY, NINE

Girls scream when they see Justin Bieber. They do the same when my brother tries to kiss them.

AMANDA, NINE

The Pope always wears white. He must hate it when it's spaghetti Bolognese for dinner in case he spills the sauce down his white top. My mum tells me off if I do that, but the Pope's lucky: he doesn't have a mum to nag him about eating tidily. The cardinals probably tell him off though.

ADAM, EIGHT

The Pope doesn't have a real job. It takes up all his time being Pope and learning about sin. I suppose if he was short of money he could get a part-time job, like a paper round. He could maybe fit that in around church services.

JONATHAN, NINE

Bruce Forsyth was given a knighthood by the Queen. But he wasn't like a proper knight. He didn't arrive at Buckingham Palace on horseback and wearing armour.

MICHAEL, FIVE

DEAR GOD ...

Some schoolchildren were asked to write a letter to the Almighty. They're still waiting for a reply, but that's the postal service for you!

Dear God, did you mean for the giraffe to look like that or was it an accident?

NORMA, FIVE

Please let Uncle Sid in to heaven when he dies. I know Auntie Beatie isn't happy about his new lady friend, but he has always been good to me and never forgets my birthday.

JACQUELINE, SIX

Please fix it for Aunt Rhona to get a razor for Christmas so that I don't have to kiss her hairy face the next time she comes to stay.

NICHOLAS, SEVEN

If you give me a genie lamp like Aladdin, I will give you anything you want, except my money and my chess set.
RAPHAEL, SIX

You must be very, very old. Madonna is very old too and I think you'd be nice together, but I think she is married to Jesus.
SARAH, SIX

If you can't make me a better boy, don't worry about it. I'm having a real good time like I am.
LEROY, FIVE

please let Grandma in to heaven because she is very kind. She is not well, though, so if I were you I would start getting her room ready soon.
CAITLIN, FIVE

Is there a supermarket in heaven? Because that's where Grandma always shops, and she'll be very upset if there isn't one.
AMANDA, SIX

Is it true that my dad won't get to heaven if he uses his bowling words in the house?
ANITA, FIVE

When I go to heaven, please make sure I have a room with a nice view over Paradise, and not one facing a car park or something. Because that's what happened to us when we went to Florida last year.
SAMANTHA, SIX

When I get to heaven, will you help me make friends as I'm afraid none of my family will be there?
CATHERINE, SIX

Is there anyone in heaven where you can go for a walk because my grandma likes walking? Are there footpaths on the clouds?
SHARLEEN, SEVEN

Is it always sunny in heaven? Grandma wants to know if she needs to pack factor 15 sun cream.
KAYLEIGH, EIGHT

Is there lots to do in heaven? Because my grandad likes golf, so I hope there's a course. Do you play? What's your handicap?

PAUL, SEVEN

If when I get to heaven I don't like it, can you send me back down to earth? I'd be quite happy just to be a cleaner or something.

LORRAINE, SEVEN

When she dies, please make sure my mummy goes to heaven and not the other place because she doesn't like going anywhere that's too hot. That's why we always have to go on holiday to boring Wales and not Spain.

ANTONY, EIGHT

Now that my grandpa is in heaven, please make sure he doesn't smoke because that's what killed him down here, too.

CYNDI, SIX

When I die, I've decided that I want to come back as President of the United States. I thought I'd ask you early because you probably get a lot of people asking for the same thing and I know you can't make them all President.

RAMON, EIGHT

My turtle died. We buried her in our yard. Is she there with you now? If so, she really likes lettuce.

LORI, FIVE

🐟

There has been no scientific evidence put forward to affirm your existence. Please can you prove you exist?

STEPHANIE, SEVEN

🐟

My dog Bowser is getting really old now. He gets up slowly and doesn't keep up with me any more when we run. Mummy says he's going to die one day. Could you just make him a puppy again instead?

PATRICK, SIX

If you watch me in church on Sunday, I will show you my new shoes.

MICKEY, FIVE

I have a spelling test on Tuesday. I never get all
the words right. Maybe you could help me this time.
Or is that cheating?

MARSHALL, SIX

I have poo in my pants. Please don't tell Mrs Davies.

LAURIE, SIX

Please can you fix it for a terrible plague to strike
Bear Creek, Alabama, next week so I can have two days
off school?

DYLAN, SEVEN

My teacher Mrs Davies says if I'm bad I will go to
hell, but I want to because Grandpa lives there and it
will be fun.

DAISY, SIX

Is hell really that bad or do you just spend more on
advertising?

KARL, NINE

LOGISTICS

In school they told us what you do. Who does it when you are on vacation?
JANE, SIX

Did you really create the world in six days or did you have help?
LORRAINE, SIX

Are you really invisible or is that just a trick?
LUCY, SIX

Do you throw lightning down at us? It scares me a lot when it goes BOOM. Please stop it.
ANNE, FIVE

Why did you make snakes and spiders? I'm afraid of them.
ALICE, FIVE

Does Satan ever send you a Christmas card, or do you not speak to each other at all?

CLAUDIA, SEVEN

I bet it's very hard for you to love everybody in the whole world. There are only four people in our family and I can never do it.

NAN, FIVE

I lost my school bag last week and Mummy was very angry. Do you know where it is?

DAMIEN, FIVE

I went to this wedding and they kissed right inside the church. Is that OK?

NEIL, SIX

I didn't think orange went with purple until I saw the sunset you made on Tuesday. That was cool!

DJ, SIX

I love Jesse a lot. When I told him, he pushed me down and made my cry. Mummy says he must like me, too. What do you think?

ANGELIQUE, FIVE

Please put another holiday between Christmas and Easter. There is nothing good in there now.

GINNY, FIVE

When I get big I want to play basketball. Maybe you can make my skin black so I can play better. Also, make me really tall, too.

CHRISTOPHER, SIX

Can you make me run faster than Usain Bolt or at least faster than my brother?

STEVEN, SEVEN

Please can you fix it for me to win the next series of Britain's Got Talent? I can play 'Jingle Bells' on the paper and comb.

DIONNE, SIX

A LAW UNTO THEMSELVES

Kids are naughty and they'll test the patience of even the most experienced parent. Their neat line in excuses almost makes up for the fact they've been very, very bad.

EXCUSES, EXCUSES

Have you had an accident that wasn't your fault? Have you been blamed for someone else's wrong-doing? When you're an adult 'you could be in line for up to $50,000 compensation just by calling this number', but when you're a child it's just tough luck.

Mum, I didn't break the vase with Grandma's ashes in. She did it while trying to get out. She didn't like it in there.

SPENCER, SEVEN

I didn't break the vase at Mrs Johnson's house, but even if I had there's nothing to worry about because she said it's priceless.

TIM, SEVEN

I didn't break the vase. It just fell down. I think it was something to do with gravity — we've been studying it in science.

RUDI, NINE

How do you know it was me who broke the window? It could have been an overweight bird or a meteorite.
JASON, EIGHT

I didn't do it of my own free will. My brother hypnotized me to do it.
KRIS, EIGHT

But, Mum, it wasn't my fault the football went through the window. I didn't mean to kick it that way. I can't help it if Dad hasn't taught me to play very well.
PHILIP, SEVEN

I didn't set the chair on fire, Mum. It was already on fire when I sat in it.
BILLY, FOUR

It wasn't me who spilled tea on your book, Mum. It must have been that ghost I told you about the other week — you know, the one who flooded the bathroom, damaged Dad's geraniums, tore the wallpaper in the lounge, broke the washing machine and got ink on my bed sheets.
DANIEL, TEN

IT WASN'T ME, MUM

Honest, Mum, it wasn't me who ate those prawns off the counter, it was the cat. Look in her tummy if you don't believe me.

KELLY, SIX

What makes you think that's a small handprint on the icing? It could just as easily be a large pawprint.

JEROME, EIGHT

It's not my fault the dog got out. He must have learned how to pull out the chain on the front door, push down the handle, pull it with his teeth, turn the key in the porch door and then use his paw to press down the safety latch. After all, he is a clever dog. You know how good he is at fetching a stick.

JIMMY, TEN

I just wanted to see how much toilet paper would
actually fit in the toilet.
JACK, FOUR

I'm just feeding the bushes, like Daddy did last night
after he had all that beer.
STANLEY, FIVE

🙂

I'm not farting. I'm just burping out my bum.
DUNCAN, SIX

🙂

Don't be cross with me, Mum! I only threw water over
Grandma because I heard her say her ears were burning.
LIZZIE, SIX

The reason I didn't brush my teeth this morning is
because I read that it's important to save water.
RAPHAEL, EIGHT

Why do I need to wash behind my ears?
Nothing ever happens there.
ARCHIE, FIVE

I CAN'T GO TO BED YET

Finding a cure for the common cold, splitting the atom, working out a peace process for the Middle East – these are all simple challenges compared to persuading a reluctant child that it's time for bed.

If you make me go to sleep now, Mum, I'll wake up too early in the morning and then I'll come in and disturb you and you'll be grumpy all day.

PETRA, SIX

When I want to watch a TV show with my parents past my bedtime, my mum always sends me to bed no matter how much I fake being 'absorbed' in the programme.

REBECCA, ELEVEN

If you make me go to bed now, Mum, the dog will have nobody to play with and then he'll pester you for the rest of the evening and stop you watching your favourite show, the one with those handsome doctors.

RAMONA, SEVEN

I can't go to bed yet, Mum — I need to plan what to
buy you for your birthday.
JESSICA, SIX

I can feel one of my dizzy spells coming along . . .
soon . . . be patient.
JULIAN, EIGHT

Isn't it supposed to be bad for you to go to bed on a full
stomach? ... Yes, I know dinner was three hours ago but my
digestive system is obviously working very slowly today.
NEIL, NINE

If I have to go to bed now, Mum, there's more time for
me to go sleepwalking, and you know how dangerous
that can be. I could walk through the glass door and
then you'd have to take me to hospital. And you wouldn't
want that on your conscience, would you?
ROCHELLE, NINE

I can't walk to my bedroom. I can't walk anywhere.
My legs are out of power.
BENEDICT, SIX

SOURCES

BOOKS

Tibballs, Geoff (ed.) *Kids Say the Funniest Things*, Granada, 2000

Tibballs, Geoff (ed.) *The Mammoth Book of Jokes*, Constable & Robinson, 2006

WEBSITES

www.tiggyblog.com

www.entertainmentquotes.tribe.net

www.thestir.cafemom.com

www.firelady40.com

www.butlerwebs.com